# Sushi for Everyone

*With Master Sushi Chef*
*Andy F. Matsuda*

**Sushi Chef Institute**

Text and photographs by
Chef Andy F. Matsuda
William Royal McLane

# Table of Contents

# Table of Contents

# FORWARD

Like so many of us living here in the Western world having experienced Japanese food in restaurants, I wanted to know how and if I could prepare these meals at home. I first contacted Chef Matsuda at the Sushi Chef Institute wanting to learn how to make more advanced sushi rolls than I was currently doing for my friends and family. Chef Matsuda suggested that I come to his classes to learn not just about rolls, but also about the entire Japanese menu. Subsequently I completed both the professional I and professional II courses at the Sushi Chef Institute in Little Tokyo, downtown Los Angeles, and an apprenticeship at the Matsuda family restaurant Masunomi Matsuya in Nishiwaki, Japan near Osaka. During my course of study I took extensive notes and photographs of each dish that I learned.

After returning home from my studies I realized that I had a pictorial essay of the Sushi Chef Institute curriculum as well as step by step notes for each recipe. Or what amounted to a testimonial to Chef Matsuda's sensibility and mastery of his craft as well as his expertise as a teacher. I suggested using these notes and photographs as a basis for a textbook. With Chef Matsuda's cooperation and technical assistance we have completed this first textbook for the Sushi Chef Institute. The text book is structured as follow: First the basic ingredients, knives, utensils, and various cooking techniques for each recipe as well as sashimi and sushi preparation. As noted above, the notes on the recipes and the majority of the photographs were taken while participating in class, preparing each dish as I learned it, and practicing to acquire the sensibility of Japanese presentation. So if there is a photo that could be sharper or an explanation clearer, the faults are all my own and absolutely no reflection on Chef Matsuda-san.

Whether you want to add a Japanese touch to your meals at home or are contemplating a career as a sushi chef, Chef Matsuda and the Sushi Chef Institute are dedicated to unveiling the secrets to your success. If you do not have the time, the money, or the ability to travel to Los Angeles to attend the Sushi Chef Institute you have in your hands a pictorial guide and step by step explanation of the curriculum. This textbook offers every cook at home or professional the opportunity to share in this great culinary tradition. For information about the Sushi Chef Institute, visit *www.sushischool.net*.

*W. R. McLane*
*Calgary, Alberta 2007*

# A message from chef Matsuda:

Eating is a most basic activity; however, many of us are forgetting how to eat. In our busy lives we easily forget how lucky we are to enjoy good health. Often, it is only when illness strikes, that we learn how important our health is to our lives. Eating well requires knowing what foods we need to eat, how to choose them, and how to prepare them. If you understand mother nature's love you will become a great chef and a healthy human. By making the right choices in daily eating behavior you can greatly improve the overall quality of your health; and life in general. Life is too short, so make the best of it!

# INTRODUCTION

Master Chef Andy Matsuda started his career as a teenager working in his family's restaurant near Kobe, Japan. He then worked at one of the most prestigious restaurants in Osaka for five years honing his skills. He moved to Los Angeles when he was twenty-five years old bringing only his sushi knives and his hopes and dreams. Speaking no English at that time, he landed his first job in Little Tokyo in downtown Los Angeles as an assistant chef. Within a week Andy was promoted to chief sushi chef. Since then, Chef Matsuda has worked at fine sushi restaurants in Los Angeles, Aspen, New York, and has also had the opportunity of working for major hotels learning to cook other ethnic cuisines such as French and Italian. He is also a consultant to the Japanese restaurant business providing insight and expertise to many new restaurant owners.

At the age of thirty-six, Chef Matsuda was diagnosed with cancer and he began a battle for his life. After four years of intensive treatments and self-reflection, he attained a new understanding of the relationship between food and part health, people and their environment. Upon overcoming cancer, Chef Matsuda was full of appreciation and wanted to pay back his debt of gratitude to American society by sharing his years of experience, knowledge, and skill with all people, to hold back no secrets, and to unveil the mysticism that has shrouded the art of sushi making for centuries.

Chef Matsuda opened the Sushi Chef Institute in 2002 to teach the beauty of Japanese cuisine. This is his gift to America. In the words of Chef Matsuda, "I would like to impart my knowledge of sushi to all people in an accurate, comprehensive manner in order for them to discover new aspects of cuisine and to gain more interest in sushi. Also through this food culture, I would like to teach and pass on my way of blessing nature, love among individuals, and peace among countries. My teaching ethic is based on an appreciation of nature, family and society.

Chef Matsuda teaches his students the Three Method which means, 'S'eason, 'S'imple, and 'S'ublime. All ingredients should be complimentary. The dishes and their presentations should reflect the season and are remarkable in their simple beauty. Sushi should not be too complicated. Sushi at its best is elegant, beautiful, yet simple, and delicious.

# Introduction

The Sushi Chef Institute offers two courses:
The first course, Professional I, teaches the fundamentals of Japanese cuisine. In the following course, Professional II, students acquire the knowledge and techniques required for making sushi. Classes meet five days a week Monday through Friday from 8:00 am until 1:00 pm. Each course of study is four weeks long. The Sushi Chef Institute is accredited by the State of California and Chef Matsuda is a state approved instructor.

In his text, Japanese Cooking: A Simple Art, Shizuo Tsuji has this to say:

Japanese cuisine is deceptively simple. There are two main ingredients: a rather delicate stock, *dashi*, made from *konbu* (giant kelp) and flakes of dried bonito, and *shoyu*, Japanese soy sauce. There are two key requirements: pristine freshness and prime condition of materials used, and beauty of presentation. The ideal formal meal progression is from clear soup and *sashimi* through entrees of grilled, steamed, simmered, and fried foods to conclude with rice and pickles - and sometimes *miso* soup - followed by tea and fruit. The traditional basic formula, however, is much simpler - '*ichiju sansai*,' or soup and three. That is, a soup and three main dishes: 1. Fresh, uncooked fish; *sashimi*, 2. A grilled dish; *yaki-mono*, 3. A simmered dish; *ni-mono*. This is the usual composition of a meal served at home, always followed by rice, pickles, tea, and often fruit. Japanese meals always have a definite beginning, middle, and the end is always essentially rice, pickles, and tea. To achieve balance in the Japanese manner, there are two guidelines: make sure the same ingredient is not used repeatedly; secondly, let the dishes represent various cooking techniques: The 'soup and three' idea for example.

Some of the etiquette regarding chopsticks, *hashi*, is worth mentioning. It is usual to turn chopsticks around and use the handle end to serve one's self from a common dish. When eating sushi at a table, traditionally one uses chopsticks but when eating sushi at a sushi counter the fingers are used. Two absolute taboos related to chopsticks are to never stick chopsticks upright in a bowl of rice and never use your chopsticks to take something from someone else's chopsticks. These two things relate to Japanese funerary customs and must never be done while at table.

# Tools

*Wa-hocho* (Knives):

*Wa-hocho*, *Wa* - Japanese, *Hocho* - Knife. Japanese knives are beveled on one side only and are sharpened using a whetstone. Each knife shape and style has a specific purpose in the Japanese kitchen.

The three primary knives used in the Sushi Chef Institute kitchen are:

*Deba* - a kitchen cleaver.

*Yanagi* - for slicing fish.

*Usuba* - vegetable knife.

A complete set of knives and tools.

The knives are sharpened using a whetstone and *Sabitori*.

## Six Main Ingredients

*Sake*, Soy sauce, Salt, Sugar, *Mirin*, and Vinegar; the "Mother Ingredients" for many sauces. *Sake* is a rice wine made by fermentation in two transactions. *Mirin* is a sweet rice wine used in cooking. Rice vinegar is acidic and used for marinating and preserving. Salt: land based salt are 99.9% sodium and stay in suspension when mixed in liquid. Ocean sea salt is 98% sodium and 2% minerals and dissolves into solution when mixed in liquid. Ocean salt is the healthier choice. Sugar used is of the cane variety.

Four types of soy sauce are used:
- Dark - is used especially in the Tokyo area.
- Light - is saltier; found more in Osaka and Kyoto areas.
- *Tamari* - is sweeter and is used in sauces such as eel sauce.
- White - is used for clarity and color considerations.

Pictured is *mirin*, *sake*, rice vinegar, dark and light soy sauce, sesame seeds, *wasabi*, bottled *sushi-zu*, green tea, *nori*, and short grain rice.

## *Kaiseki*

*Kai* - heart and stomach, *Seki* - stone.
*Kaiseki* is inspired by the Buddhist tradition of placing a warm stone against the abdomen to stave off hunger. In modern Japanese cuisine *Kaiseki* is the idea of just enough food and tea to satisfy but not over indulge. The basic *Kaiseki* concept is in season, simple, and sublime - not too much, nor over decorated.

# Stock

Primary *dashi*. Pour 1 gallon of fresh water into a large sauce pan. Place a 5 square inch piece of *konbu* kelp in the cold water then bring to the boil. Remove the kelp, shock the hot water by adding 1/4 cup cold water, add 5 grams of bonito flakes and remove from heat. Let stand for a minimum 5 minutes, then strain the liquid. The kelp and bonito flakes can be reused for secondary *dashi* by repeating the procedure for primary *dashi*. Secondary *dashi* is often used for *miso* soup stock. Primary *dashi* is used for clear soup, sauces, simmering stocks, etc. Primary *dashi* is made each day as it does not keep well. When making *dashi* for dipping sauces extra bonito flakes are used.

# Soups

*Sui-mono* (Clear soup for cleansing the palate):
Clear soup uses *dashi*, *sake*, light color soy sauce, and salt; all ingredients are added to taste. Clear soup should be subtle.

Traditionally, Clear soup contains 3 items:
- *Wanko*, the main item;
  shrimp for example.
- *Sui-kuchi*, a floating item;
  julienne of carrot and *daikon*.
- *Ko-no-mono*, an accent;
  a twist of lemon zest.

*Miso* Soup:
Uses Primary or Secondary *dashi*, *mirin*, soy, and salt. *Miso* soup can be a hearty soup containing several ingredients or a simple soup containing 3 items as in *sui-mono*.

*Miso* soup proportions for 1 serving are:
    8 oz *dashi*
    1/2 oz *miso* (heaping teaspoon)
    1 tsp *mirin*
    salt and soy to taste

## Mother Vinegar Sauces

Two flavor vinegar sauce, *Nihai-zu*: Vinegar - soy (dark or light) - *Dashi* or water.

    1/2 cup vinegar
    2/3 cup *dashi* or water
    2 Tbls dark or light soy.

Also added to mother vinegar sauces are grated vegetables, fruits, or pre-packaged products. Pre-packaged products include chili paste, plum sauce, *wasabi*, *miso* paste, etc.

Examples:
    vinegar
    dark soy
    water or *dashi*
    grated cucumber and/or grated ginger

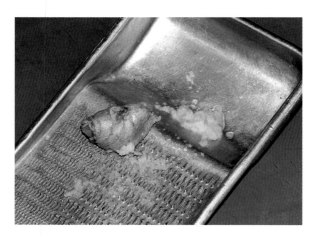

    vinegar
    light soy
    water
    Grated *daikon*

    vinegar
    dark soy
    *dashi*
    red chili paste and/or grated cucumber

    vinegar
    dark soy
    water
    red chili paste and/or sesame oil

Three flavor vinegar sauce *Sanbai-zu*, uses the addition of *mirin* or sugar.

    1/2 cup vinegar
    2/3 cup *dashi* or water
    2 Tbls dark or light soy
    1 1/2 Tbls sugar or *mirin*

There are endless variations when creating vinegar sauces. To this basic recipe mentioned above, one can add a number of ingredients, such as: sesame chili oil and/or grated cucumber can be added, as well as any of the other fruits, vegetables, or pre-packaged products. Be creative!

Sweet Vinegar:
    1 part rice vinegar
    1 part sugar or *mirin*
    1 part *dashi*

Dissolve the sugar in (or mix the *mirin* with) the vinegar then add *dashi* or water. Bring just to a boil, remove from heat, and cool to room temperature. Keeps indefinitely refrigerated.

Sauces play an important role in sushi making, providing variation and flare; while the different colors create contrast in the presentation.

*Wasabi* sauce (light green):
    *wasabi* paste - 1 part
    mayonnaise - 1 part
    dash of *mirin*

*Wasabi* #2:
    sour cream - 1 part
    *wasabi* paste - 1 part
    sugar
    dash of *mirin* and *yuzu* (citrus)

Green spicy sauce (blended):
    jalapeños (seeded) - 10
    cilantro - one bunch
    garlic (crushed) - 5 cloves
    olive oil
    salt and pepper to taste

*Miso* dressing:
    vinegar - 1 part
    oil - 3 part
    white *miso* - 1 part
    sugar - 1 (adjust to taste)
    salt and pepper to taste
    dash *yuzu* (citrus) if desired

Spicy Mayonnaise (light red):
    mayonnaise - 2 part
    sriracha - 1 part
    honey or *mirin* - 1 part

Sour cream/mustard sauce (yellow):
    sour cream - 2 part
    mustard - 1 part (mustard powder mixed in water)
    honey - 1 part

Red sauce:
    sriracha - 2 part
    honey - 1 part

Mix *miso*, sugar, salt and pepper with vinegar, then drizzle oil slowly while whisking continuously.

*Ponzu* Sauce:
A light yet tangy citrus and soy sauce dip widely used as a dressing for vinegared foods (*su-no-mono*) and with one-pot dishes such as *shabu-shabu*. *Ponzu* is also widely used as a dipping sauce for white fish *sashimi*. The proportions are:
    1 part *daidai* (citrus)
    1 part soy
    1 part vinegar
    1 part *mirin*
    1/2 part *tamari*
    *konbu* kelp (in the container)

Age a minimum of 2 weeks for best flavor.
The *konbu* in the storage container mellows and enriches the sauce.
*Ponzu* mixed with sesame oil and mustard is a good sauce to use for searing.

## *Zensai*: Appetizers

- *Renkon* chips:         Lotus root chips thinly sliced, marinated in 5% vinegar and water solution, then dry and deep fried twice.
- *Temari imo*:         Sweet potato ball.
- *Nishiki tamago*:         Two color egg.
- *Ebi shinjo*:         Shrimp stuffed mushrooms, deep fried.
- *Ebi kimi-zu*:         Shrimp with vinegar.
- *Daikon* treasure box.

*Temari imo*:

Peel steamed sweet potatoes then press the potatoes through a fine sieve. Mix 80% mashed sweet potato with 20% green tea powder; set aside. Form the mashed sweet potatoes into 1 inch balls.

Make a small indentation in the top of the balls then place a dab of the green tea / sweet potato mixture in the indentation. Now wrap the ball in a piece of plastic wrap and twist tightly to meld the two parts together and create texture.

*Ebi shinjo*:

Clean and de-vein shrimp, chop into pieces, pound with the back of a *deba* knife then place the shrimp in a mortar and grind into a paste with a pinch of salt. Cut out the stem of a mushroom making a pocket then stuff the mushroom with the shrimp paste. Dip the bottom of the mushroom in all purpose flour, egg wash (beaten eggs), and *panko*, (bread crumbs) then deep fry.

*Daikon* treasure box:
Chop *daikon* and carrot into 3/16 inch cubes mixing together with *masago* (jalapeño flavor). Cut a *daikon* into a 1 1/4 inch cube; cut a slice for a lid. Carefully cut out the interior of the *daikon* cube creating a box. Dip the *daikon* box in salt water then fill with the *daikon*/carrot/*masago* mixture.

*Naruto hirame*:
Halibut roll. Roll together a thin strip of *daikon*, two thin pieces of halibut, a *shiso* leaf, and *yama-gobo* (pickled burdock).

*Nishiki tamago*:
Separate the whites and yolks from 5 five hard boiled eggs; press the whites and yolks separately through a fine sieve. Add 2 tablespoons sugar to the whites mixing well; add a pinch of salt and mix again. Now place the mixture in a rectangular pan pressing down with a fork. Then layer the yolks on top of the white's mixture in the pan. Cover with waxed paper and place in a steamer for 15 minutes.

*Renkon* (lotus root) chips:
Peel then slice the lotus root into disks. Immerse the slices in 5% vinegar and water solution for 20-30 minutes. Dry the *renkon* slices then deep fry, drain off excess oil, allow drying. Deep fry the disks a second time for crispy chips.

Vinegar in the water preserves the color of vegetables and fruit as well as prevents browning.

*Ebi kimi-zu*:

3 beaten egg yolks, 2 pinches salt, 1/2 cup sweet vinegar (1/2 cup rice vinegar, 1/2 cup *dashi*, 2 1/2 Tbls sugar or *mirin*. Dissolve sugar or mix *mirin* in the vinegar then add the *dashi*. Bring to a boil, remove from heat, cool to room temperature).

Place the ingredients in a sauce pan over medium low heat stirring constantly. Do not burn or over heat causing the egg yolks to skin over. A double boiler is helpful. As the sauce begins to bubble and thicken, take care stirring constantly. Now pour the sauce through a fine sieve and place in the refrigerator to cool. Steam the cleaned shrimp for three minutes. Marinate steamed shrimp for a minute or two in sweet vinegar marinade. Arrange two marinated steamed shrimp together (which represents happiness and togetherness) on a plate. Serve in a "pool" of the hollandaise sauce or on a *shiso* leaf with a little of the sauce.

An appetizer presentation for one person.

An appetizer presentation for two persons.

*Kikka daikon* (Chrysanthemum *daikon*):

Peel the *daikon*, slice in rounds +/- 3/4 inch thick. Stand the *daikon* on one end. Cross slice as deeply and as finely as possible. Placing the *daikon* between two bamboo chopsticks will allow you to cut to a maximum depth without cutting completely through the *daikon*. Marinate first in 5% saltwater solution then rinse in fresh water. Place the *daikon* in a zip lock plastic bag with sweet vinegar and chili peppers. Place the plastic bag with the *daikon* in a bowl; place another slightly smaller bowl on top adding weight. Place in the refrigerator for two or three days then remove the weight placing the *daikon* in a suitable closed container with sweet vinegar, *konbu*, and whole red chilies.

*Horenso ohitashi*:

Boiled spinach and soy. Wash spinach then gather in a bunch binding the stems with a rubber band. First, dip just the stems in boiling water until they begin to soften. Now allow the leaves to be immersed along with the stems for several seconds, then immerse the spinach in ice water for 30 seconds. Lay the spinach in a *makisu* (*sushi* bamboo mat) and wring the excess water out of the spinach. Now roll the spinach in a 1:1:1 *dashi*, *mirin*, soy sauce mixture then squeeze out the excess liquid.

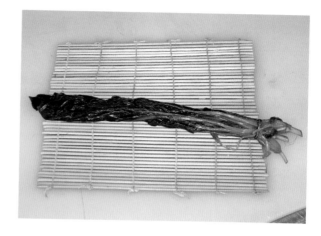

Next, slice the spinach bundle into 1 1/2 inch long sections and stack in a bowl. Cut one section into two 3/4 inch lengths and press one end of each length in sesame seeds; stand upright in the bowl with the stacked pieces. Garnish with bonito flakes then add a little of the *dashi*, *mirin*, and soy sauce mixture to the bowl.

*Ao-negi nuta*:
Green onions and *Miso*.
    90 grams white *miso*
    60 grams sugar
    1 Tbsp *sake*
    1 Tbsp *mirin*
    1 Tbsp vinegar
    1 Tbsp light soy sauce
    1/2 tsp hot mustard powder paste

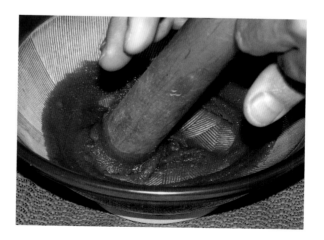

Place the *miso*, sugar, *sake*, *mirin* and soy in a mortar and blending together with the pestle. Now add the vinegar and continue to mix thoroughly. Add a pinch of salt and mix well. Add the hot mustard and mix well.

Set the mixture aside. Place one bunch of green onions, bulb end first, in boiling water until the bulbs soften. Then allow the greens to be immersed with the bulbs until the onions are tender. Immerse immediately in ice water for 30 seconds. Remove and lay the onions flat on a cutting board. Use a chopstick to roll the excess moisture out of the onions. Roll from the bulb end toward the tops.

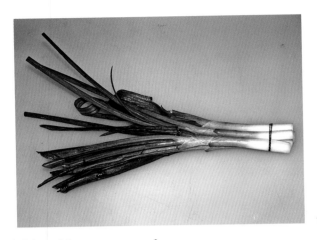

Now fold an onion at the bulb end and wrap with the greens to form a bite sized morsel. Mix the onion wraps in the miso sauce, place in a bowl, and sprinkle with sesame seeds.

Cucumber *su-no-mono*:
Slice cucumber in thin half-rounds and soak in water with 5% sea salt for 10 minutes. Rinse in clear water, add *wakame*, sesame seeds, and grated lemon or lime zest. A little sweet vinegar can be added if desired. A dressing using 1 part vinegar, 1 part *mirin*, 1 part *dashi*, and a pinch of salt can be used.
Add thinly sliced *Tako* if desired.

## *Men Mono*: Noodles

*Somen* (rice noodles), *Soba* (buckwheat noodles), *Udon* (wheat noodles). Dipping sauces are *dashi*, *mirin*, and light soy sauce. Cold dipping sauce proportions are 4 parts *dashi*, 1 part *mirin*, and 1 part dark soy sauce. Hot dipping sauce proportions are 10:1:1 Ground chilies can be added to the hot dipping sauces.

Other ingredients that can be added to the dipping sauces are:
    *sarashi-negi* (rinsed, chopped green onions) and grated ginger; or
    *sarashi-negi* and *wasabi*, *kizami-nori* (julienne seaweed); or
    *sarashi-negi* and grated ginger, *kizami-nori*.
    (for more information on *sarashi-negi* see pages 15 and 40)

*Soba* noodles:
Boil the noodles then immerse them in ice water.
When serving soba noodles hot, it is still necessary to shock the noodles in ice water to retain the proper texture, then dip them again briefly in the hot water to reheat.

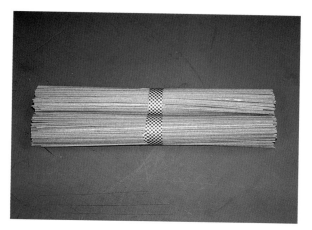

*Soba* noodles are pictured here arranged on a *makisu* and garnished with *kizami-nori* (*nori* julienne). Serve cold with a dipping sauce. After eating the noodles, add some of the hot water that the noodles were boiled in to the remaining dipping sauce to create a delicious soup.

# Men Mono

*Udon* noodles:
Serve hot in the 10:1:1 dipping sauce with an egg swirled around in the sauce, add fried tofu (*inari*), green onion, and a little ground chili.
Or serve noodles cold with the dipping sauce on the side.

*Somen* noodles:
Two ways to boil *somen* noodles are simply to dump the noodles in boiling water or wrap a rubber band around one end of the bunch of noodles to keep them together which becomes an aid to presentation.
For example: Cut off the rubber band end of the noodles after cooking, then cut the remaining length of noodles in 3 equal sections. Fold each section in half; serve in an ice water bath with carrot star garnish and a dipping sauce on the side.

*Sarashi-negi*:
Place chopped green onion in a cheese cloth;
rinse under cold water while squeezing out the gooey liquid that forms.
This process will make the onions milder.
(See page 40)

# Curry

Cut carrots and potatoes in 3/4 inch irregular shapes. Cut a yellow onion in half then slice; thinly slice a garlic clove. Melt 2 Tbls of butter in a frying pan; add the garlic and onion and sauté over medium heat until translucent.
Add 1/2 cup beef strips, the carrots and potatoes. Stir well then add stock (beef, chicken, or *dashi*). Now pour all the ingredients into a stock pot, bring to a boil, then reduce heat to a strong simmer until all ingredients are tender.
Now add 1 1/2 blocks of the curry stirring well. Grate (very fine) 3-4 Tbls of apple into the pot

and 1/2 Tsp of ginger while continuing to simmer. Salt to taste, add 2 tsp of light soy sauce stirring well. Serve with rice or *udon* noodles in a 10:1:1 sauce.

# *Okonomi-yaki*

Japanese mountain yam grated very fine becomes a starchy liquid. Place 1/2 cup into a bowl, add 1 beaten egg, 1 cup sifted flour, and 1/2 cup *dashi*; stir well using a wire whisk. Add water if necessary for consistency, add salt, then set aside. Julienne green cabbage and cut julienne strips into shorter lengths; place in a mixing bowl. Add chopped green onions, beef strips, and some of the mountain yam batter; mix well. Heat 1 Tbls vegetable oil in a frying pan, add the vegetable and beef mixture to the pan frying on both sides until done.

To serve: Place the "pancake" on a plate, pour vegetable and fruit sauce (*ton-katsu* sauce) over the top, sprinkle with bonito flakes, seaweed flakes, and chopped green onions. This dish is often served as a snack. Shrimp, squid, pork, chicken, most anything can be used in this recipe.

## Chicken

The "Oyster" muscles on the back of the chicken are key areas. The thigh and leg are removed together with the oyster muscle from the back then de-boned and used as one whole piece, which is considered the most interesting meat on the chicken by the Japanese. The breast and wing are taken together then the tenderloin is removed from the underside of the breast. The wing joint is revealed and the wing is split off.

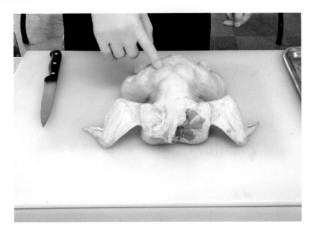

The first wing section is skinned and the meat cut down the bone and rolled over one end so you have a bite size morsel of meat with a "handle." The second wing joint is done in the same fashion by removing the small bone and rolling the meat down over the end of the larger bone. The third wing joint is used for stock.

The breast is skinned then cut length wise into two pieces. Cut each piece partially through down the center and fold out into a thin filet. The wish bone and tail are cut off of the skeleton. The bones, skin, and skeleton are used for stock.

Chicken stock is made with unpeeled sliced ginger, sliced garlic, water, the bones, skin, and skeleton. The tenderloin pieces and the breast before dividing are pictured on the left, while the entire de-boned chicken is pictured here on the right.

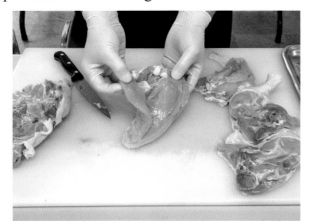

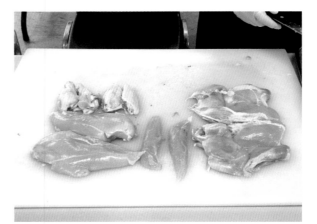

*Yaki-tori*:

Mix salt 60% and pepper 40% in a bowl.
Using thigh and leg meat cut into bite sized pieces
placing them on a bamboo skewer.
Soak the skewers in water for several minutes
before using to prevent them from burning. Sprinkle
with the salt and pepper mixture then place on a
grill over an open flame. Serve with a dash of
*yuzu* pepper.

*Teri-yaki* is a U.S. dish which is called *Jibu-ni* in Japan. *Jibu-ni* style uses a 60% *mirin*, 40% dark soy sauce mixture. Heat 1 Tbls vegetable oil in a frying pan. Sprinkle thigh and leg meat with salt and pepper, dredge in flour, then sauté in the frying pan. When the chicken is cooked through pour in several Tbls of the *mirin*/soy mixture; reduce to thicken. Remove the chicken, cut into bite sized pieces, place on a plate, pour the sauce reduction over the top. Garnish with a little vegetables and serve.

*Jibu-ni* style is prepared one serving at a time. Where many servings must be prepared, U.S. style *teri-yaki* is the recipe to use.

*Teri-yaki*: Good for multiple servings.
The sauce:
    2 parts chicken stock
    1 part soy sauce
    1 part *mirin*
    1/2 part sugar
    1/2 part *tamari*
    salt to taste

If desired, add about 1 clove each sliced ginger and garlic while cooking. Place ingredients in a sauce pan, bring to the boil, and add potato starch water *katakuriko* to thicken. Pour in the potato starch water stirring constantly until the desired thickness is achieved.
Potato starch water: 2 Tbls potato starch - 2 Tbls water.

# Chicken

The chicken:
Sprinkle thigh and leg meat with salt and pepper mixture then grill or pan fry.
To serve, Cut the chicken into bite sized pieces, place on a plate, and spoon *teri-yaki* sauce over the top.
Use the same sauce for *teri-yaki* salmon, beef, etc.

*Tatsuta-age*:
Ginger, dark soy sauce, potato starch (*Katakuriko*).
Place together in a bowl 1 Tbls finely grated ginger and 2 Tbls dark soy. Marinate the chicken breast for a few minutes in the ginger soy mixture then dredge in potato starch. Deep fry at 350°F for (+/-) 10 minutes.
To test the oil for correct temperature, place the ends of wooden chopsticks down in the oil.
Bubbles should form around the ends of the chopsticks but the oil should not smoke (too hot).
Drain chicken pieces on paper to absorb any excess oil. The pieces should look crispy golden with flecks of white snow on them (from the potato starch).
Serve with lemon garnish.

*Oyako donburi*:
Sauce: 4 *dashi*, 1 dark soy sauce, 1 *mirin*.
Other ingredients: 1 beaten egg, green onion sliced diagonally, yellow onion cut in half and sliced, breast meat of chicken or tender-loin pieces thinly sliced (not too thin nor cubed as cubes take too long to cook).
Place chicken pieces in a *donburi* pan with the *dashi*, *mirin*, soy mixture. Layer yellow onion slices on top; cover then simmer until the chicken is tender. Now layer on the green onion and pour in the beaten egg; cover and cook briefly (egg should still be runny).
Serve in a bowl over rice.

## *Tamago* (Eggs):

*Kinshi tamago* (egg sheet):

1 beaten egg; oil the square *tamago* pan over medium heat. Drain off any excess oil and wipe pan with a paper towel evenly covering the bottom and sides of the pan with oil. Pour in the egg at the top of the pan then tilt the pan toward the handle to spread the egg evenly across the bottom of the pan. Cook until the eggs are dry enough to lift the top left corner of the egg sheet, tilt the pan up while blowing gently on the edge of the egg to lift it off the bottom of the pan. Catch the egg sheet on your chopsticks and gently turn the sheet over in the pan and cook for 10-15 seconds. Then invert the pan over a paper towel allowing the egg sheet to lay flat on the paper towel.

*Kinshi tamago* is also used in *sushi* rolls for added interest and color. Chopping the egg sheet into julienne as an addition to *gunkan sushi* and *chirashi sushi* is also done frequently. Pictured here the *kinshi tamago* is used to wrap a mixture of *sushi* rice, *tobiko*, chopped *shiso* leaf or cilantro, and sesame seeds. *Ebi* or *unangi* is added as well.

Use a *hachimaki* around the *kinshi* wrap or slice into two pieces for presentation.

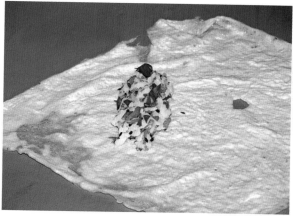

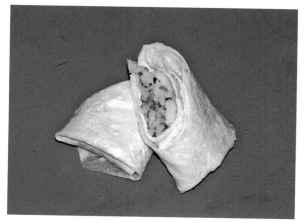

## *Tamago-yaki* (Sweet omelet):

For two omelets.
  16 eggs
  1/2 cup *dashi*
  2.5 oz sugar
  1 oz *mirin*
  1 oz *sake*
  1 oz light soy sauce
  1 pinch of salt

Mix all ingredients except the eggs in a sauce pan over low heat to melt the sugar. Beat the eggs together then add the eggs into the other ingredients mixing well. Divide the liquid into two parts to make two omelets.

To cook: Add vegetable oil to a square copper omelet pan over medium high heat. When the oil is hot, pour 1 ladle full of the egg mixture into the pan.

Cook the eggs until they begin to dry out then roll the omelet from the top of the pan toward the handle three folds. Use a paper towel saturated with vegetable oil to oil the top section of the pan, then push the folded omelet to the top of the pan and swab the lower section of the pan with oil.

Pour in another ladle full of the egg mixture. Lift the folded omelet using chopsticks to allow some of the egg mixture to flow beneath the omelet. Again, as the eggs begin to dry out, roll the omelet from the top of the pan toward the handle two or three folds.

This is done by pivoting the pan upward using the wrist as a fulcrum point and chop-sticks to help control the omelet. Repeat this process until all the egg mixture has been folded into the omelet.

Slide the omelet to each end of the pan to square the edges then place the omelet into a *makisu*.

Fold the *makisu* around the omelet to mod the omelet into shape. Serve the omelet by cutting into pieces for *nigiri sushi,* or slice into 8 pieces and serve arranged on a plate.

*Tamago* roll cutting:

Use a standard 8 egg *tamago* omelet. Cut off a 5/8 inch thick piece using an uneven motion with the knife to get a ripple effect on the face of the *tamago* piece. Cut a 5/8 inch thick slice of *tamago* then insert a knife in the center of the edge side making an incision. Then on the top face of the *neta* piece at the center, cut through to the incision at 45 degrees. Turn the *neta* piece over cutting a 45 degree angle on the bottom of the piece to finish. Or cut a 3/4 inch thick slice of *tamago* then cut a slot part way through the slice on one edge. Wrap with a piece of *nori* cut to size and tuck the ends into the slot.

Insert a small ball of rice into the slot then cut the *tamago* slice into two equal pieces through the center of the *nori* and rice ball.

22

# Beef

Beef is graded in three levels which are 1 - Prime, 2 - Choice, 3 - Select. Cows are slaughtered at two years old. For prime grade beef the cattle are grain fed during the last six months before slaughter. For choice grade beef the cattle are grain fed during the last three months, for select grade beef the cattle are grain fed during the final 1 1/2 months. Beef dishes include *Negi-maki*, *Niku-jaga*, and *Tataki*.

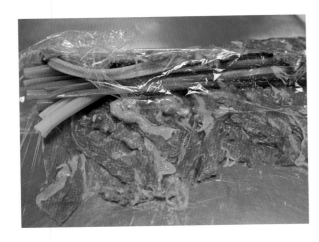

*Negi-maki*:
 Thinly sliced beef steak
 1 green onion
 2 Tbls *sake*
 4 Tbls 60% *mirin* / 40% soy sauce mixture
 flour for dredging
 1 Tbls vegetable oil

Spread very thinly sliced beef on plastic wrap (not too long, should fit in a frying pan). Slice green onion in half length wise, then in half length wise again so the onion is not too thick and will cook quickly. Layer the sliced onion on the beef; roll the beef slices around the onion. (Parboiled leeks, green beans, asparagus, etc. can also be used). Insert skewers into the beef rolls at an angle so the rolls will turn easily in the frying pan. Salt and pepper the rolls, dredge in flour, then fry over medium heat in 1 Tbs of vegetable oil. When the beef is cooked, pour 2 Tbls of *sake* over the meat (tenderizes the beef), pour in 3-4 Tbs of 60% *mirin* / 40% soy sauce mixture and simmer to reduce.

To serve: Remove the skewers then slice the roll into bite sized pieces. Pour the reduced sauce over the pieces arranged on a plate. If desired, sprinkle with sesame seeds.

Beef *Tataki*:
1 rib eye steak prime cut, excess fat removed, salt and pepper to taste; 1 Tbls vegetable oil, cucumber julienne, *ponzu* sauce. Sprinkle salt and pepper on each side of the steak. Heat a frying pan extra hot to sear in the juices. When the pan is hot, add 1 Tbls vegetable oil; place the beef steak in the pan. Sear for 30 seconds on each side then plunge the steak into ice water for 1 minute; pat dry using a cloth towel.

To serve: Slice the steak against the grain on a thin angle cut arranging the slices on top of the cucumber julienne arranged on a plate. Put a pinch of sea salt on each slice then pour *ponzu* sauce over the slices; decorate with *wasabi* sauce (1 *wasabi*, 2 mayonnaise), add chopped green onion and julienne of ginger (hot chilies or cilantro may also be used), finish with a dab of red chili paste.

*Niku-jaga*:

Thinly sliced beef steak cut into 1 1/2 inch squares, 2 medium potatoes cut in 1 1/2 inch cubes, 1 yellow onion cut in half and sliced, 1/2 cup *sake*, 1/2 cup *mirin*, 2 Tbls light soy sauce, 1 Tbls vegetable oil.

Sauté the yellow onion slices in a frying pan then add the beef; sauté for 1 minute. Add potato pieces, the *sake*, and *mirin*. Cover with a small plate that will apply weight to the ingredients in the pan promoting even cooking. Simmer for 30 minutes stirring once or twice. Add the light soy sauce for the last minute or so of cooking. Serve in a bowl.

# Pork

Pork should be pink in color not white, nor too dark either. Pork dishes include *Ton-katsu* and *Katsu-don*.

*Ton-katsu*:
1/2 inch thick boneless pork loin, slice through the fibrous area at the fat back a few times to help prevent shrinking while cooking. Tenderize using the heel of the knife across the grain, turn 45 degrees and tenderize with the grain. Mix *ton-katsu* sauce and ketchup in a 1 to1 ratio with a squeeze of fresh lemon.

The marinade:
1/2 cup *sake* (helps tenderize), 1/2 cup milk (helps remove any strong odors). Marinate the pork in the *sake*/milk mixture for 10 minutes; remove and pat dry using a cloth towel. Salt and pepper each side of the pork then dredge in flour, shake off excess, immerse in 2 beaten eggs, then dredge in the *panko*, (finely ground bread crumbs). The cutlet can be frozen at this stage and cooked at a later time if desired. Place the cutlet in a deep fryer at 350°F degrees cooking until golden brown.

To serve:
Cut into bite sized pieces, arrange on a plate, pour 2 Tbls of *ton-katsu* sauce mixture over the top. Serve with garnish, potato salad, and mustard; or with vegetables as shown in the picture.

*Katsu-don (Donburi)*:
1/2 cup 4:1:1 mixture (*dashi*, *mirin*, soy), a few slices yellow onion and chopped green onion; 1 breaded deep fried pork *ton-katsu* cutlet, 1 beaten egg, 1 serving steamed rice. Pour the 4:1:1 sauce in a *donburi* pan. Add the slices of yellow onion, bite sized pieces of the pork cutlet and simmer 3-4 minutes. Add a little chopped green onion and a beaten egg. Simmer 20-30 seconds; the egg should be runny. Pour off excess sauce; Serve in a bowl over rice.

Mashed Potato Salad:
Salt and rinse julienne carrots and cucumber; squeeze out excess moisture. Add the carrots and cucumber to mashed potatoes; combine with mayonnaise, a squeeze of fresh lemon juice mixing well.

To julienne cabbage, cut the head into sections then separate layers and press flat to present a low profile so it is not necessary to lift the knife too high when cutting.

Mustard
To make Japanese mustard from powder form, place the powder mustard in a bowl and slowly drizzle water and mix until spreadable consistency. Store in an air tight container or place the container up side down to avoid mustard paste from drying out.

## Five Cooking Techniques

- *Yaki-mono* (Grilling): The highest temperature.
- *Age-mono* (Deep Frying): The next highest temperature (330°-360°F).
- *Ni-mono* (Simmering): A medium to low cooking temperature.
- *Mushi-mono* (Steaming): The lowest temperature.
- *Nama-mono* (Raw): *Sashimi* (Page 47), etc.

Lower temperatures take longer to cook but retain the most nutrition value.

*Nama-mono (Sashimi)*

*Yaki-mono*

*Ni-mono*

*Mushi-mono*

*Age-mono*

## *Yaki-mono* (Grilling):

Grilling is cooking using the highest temperature. *Dengaku* is one of traditional grilled dish using red or white *miso* paste sauce on many different ingredients.

*Dengaku miso* sauce:
  3 oz white or red *miso*
  2 oz sugar
  1 Tbls *mirin*
  1 Tbls *sake*
  1 Tbls light soy sauce

Mix all ingredients together and make sure that sugar has dissolved completely.

*Nasu Dengaku*

*Tofu Dengaku*

*Sawara Saikyo-Yaki*:

Mix 3 white *miso* - 1 *sake* - 1 *mirin* for marinate. Marinate *Sawara* (King Mackerel) or white fish for 8 hours or over night. Grill for 8-10 minute on a salamander or broiler and reduced left over marinate *miso* sauce in a pan for extra sauce and decoration. (See photo on page 44)

*Saba Shio-Yaki*:

Fillet *Saba*, simply salt and grill on a salamander or broiler for 5-10 minute.
Serve with graded *daikon,* with *ponzu* or just soy sauce. (See photo on page 44)

## *Ni-mono* (Simmering):

Simmering sauces are generally 8 parts *dashi* - 1 part *mirin* - 1 part light soy sauce.
Before simmering oily fish such as mackerel, sear with hot water (*shimo-furi*).
When simmering fish a 5:1:1 sauce is generally used.

*Taki-awase* (Simmer and assemble):
Simmering is done at medium heat. Do not boil too hard as that breaks down the vegetables as they cook.
Parboil snow peas lightly in plain water and finish in 8:1:1 stock.

*Men-tori* (Trimming the edges):
Trim the edges of vegetables when simmering so that they retain their shape while cooking. When cutting up vegetables for simmering, keep the pieces the same size for even cooking. For squash, trim the edges and cut a cornstalk pattern on the skin.
Simmer to 70% of doneness in plain water and finish in 8:1:1 simmering stock.

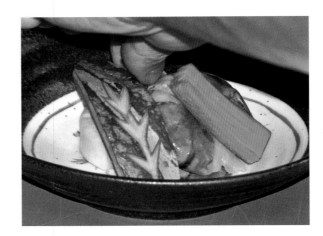

*Ebi* (Shrimp):
De-vein before parboiling (either pull out the vein from the end or insert a skewer in the shell at the third joint from the tail and pull the vein out there).
Serve with the shell on.
Finish simmering in 8:1:1 stock.

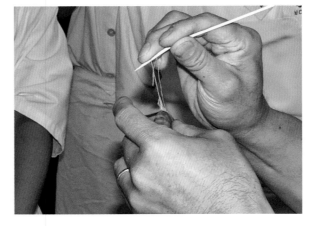

For *Tofu* put freeze dried tofu (*koya-tofu*) in hot water to soften. Shell and de-vein shrimp (raw) and cut into small pieces then pound with the back of a knife. Cut a pocket in the *tofu* and stuff with the shrimp. Chicken or fish such as salmon can also be used. Place the stuffed tofu and un-stuffed pieces in a sauce pan, add *koya-tofu* sauce (1 1/2 cups *dashi*, 2 Tbls sugar, 1 Tbls *mirin*, 2 Tbls light soy sauce, a pinch of salt);
simmer until the sauce is cooked away.

Carrot fan:

Cut a section of carrot into a rectangle, slice partially down the length several times to create a fan by opening slightly after simmering.

Bamboo shoots are pre cooked but must be parboiled to eliminate any chemicals from the packing process.

*Kuzu-an* sauce:

*Kuzu* is any starch from a root; here we are using potato starch. Use about 2 cups 8:1:1 (*dashi*, *mirin*, light soy) stock; heat in a sauce pan to the boiling point then add potato starch water to thicken. This thickened sauce is used to finish a variety of dishes.

To finish the *Taki-awase* arrange a bamboo shoot, a piece of tofu, a piece of squash, a shrimp in the shell, snow pea, and carrot fan on a rectangular plate or in a bowl. Spoon a little of the thickened 8:1:1 sauce (*kuzu-an*) over the *taki-awase* and serve.

*Furofuki-daikon*:

Cut *daikon* into 1 1/2 inch thick rounds, trim the edges and cut an X shape from the top partially down through each piece to facilitate even cooking, then simmer the *daikon* in plain water with a piece of *konbu* for up to 4-5 hours. The *daikon* should be very soft when served.

To finish: Place a piece of *daikon* in a bowl with a shrimp, carrot flower, and snow pea then spoon some of the *kuzu-an* sauce over the top.

Shown is an arrangement of *Furofuki-daikon*.

## *Mushi-mono* (Steam dishes):

*Chawan-mushi*:

3 *dashi* - 1 egg (*sake*, salt, light soy)

Use 3 parts *dashi* to 1 egg; (measure the volume of the egg, times 3 is the volume of *dashi* to use). Add a pinch of salt, 1 Tbls *mirin* or *sake*, and 1 Tbls light soy sauce. Mix all the ingredients together. Parboil bite sized pieces of chicken breast, carrot flowers, and snow peas or what you have on hand. Arrange in a cup

with a gingko nut, a piece of chicken, carrot flower, and snow pea cut in two pieces.

Add the *dashi*/egg mixture to about 70% of the cups capacity. Use a spoon to remove all of the bubbles from the surface of the liquid in the cup. Add a piece of *mitsuba* (a Japanese herb that looks like cilantro) then steam covered with waxed paper or a lid in a steamer with the lid left ajar to prevent cooking too fast. The custard is done when no liquid rises to the surface when the custard is gently pulled from the inside wall of the cup.

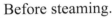

Before steaming.

After steaming.

*Temari-mushi*:

1 *dashi* - 1 egg

Use 1 egg and an equal volume of *dashi*.

The portion size is 1 egg per person. Mix *dashi* and egg then strain through a fine sieve. Line a cup or small bowl with plastic wrap, ladle in the *dashi*/egg mixture, add mushrooms, *mitsuba*, ginko nut (or what ever ingredients are available), then gather the plastic wrap to form a ball and close with a rubber band. Place back in a cup then place the cup in a steamer and steam gently to achieve a smooth glossy finished texture.

Serve in a bowl; spoon some of the thickened 8:1:1 sauce (*Kuzu-an* sauce) over the top and garnish with a carrot flower and snow pea.

*Dobin-mushi*:

Clear soup seasoned vegetables and seafood
In a teapot shaped cooker, place a shelled parboiled shrimp, mushrooms, snow pea, and *mitsuba*.
Add clear soup stock to the pot (primary *dashi*, dash of *sake*, dash of light soy, and salt to taste).
This can be cooked on a table top stove.

Steamed and simmered dishes are calming, relaxing, homey, satisfying, comforting food.

## *Age-mono* (Deep fried dishes):

*Tempura*:

The water used in *tempura* preparation is 4 cups ice water to 1 whole egg. The flour is sifted.
If no tempura flour is available use 80% all purpose flour, a dash of baking powder, and 20% potato starch or cornstarch. *Waza* brand *tempura* flour is a good product ensuring crispy *tempura*.

All ingredients must be kept cold. Oil temperature is very important and should be 170°-180°C, 330°-360°F. Vegetable oil for *tempura* can be corn oil, rice oil, salad oil, or a variety of others with up to 25% sesame oil added for flavor. *Tempura* oil should be clear not cloudy; filter or change the oil daily.

Check the oil temperature using the chopstick method:
Immerse the ends of bamboo chopsticks in the oil looking for bubbles to form at the tips; the oil should not smoke.

Another method is to drop some of the *tempura* batter into the oil; the batter should sizzle and not drop to the bottom of the pan. Remember to keep the ingredients cold to insure crispness in the final product.

*Tempura* sauce is 4 *dashi* - 1 mirin - 1 soy;
if the sauce is going to be kept for a longer period use 5:1:1. Serve the *tempura* sauce hot in a small bowl on the side with grated *daikon* and ginger. It is important to cut the vegetables the same size and thickness to ensure even cooking. Be sure to cook the denser, longer cooking vegetables first so all of the *tempura* ingredients are hot and ready to serve together. Some *tempura* ingredients are shown in the photo to the right.

To clean the shrimp remove the shell, use the back side of the knife to force excess water out of the tail, de-vein by slicing along the back of the shrimp.

Turn the shrimp over and slice across the belly at an angle in five places. Turn the shrimp back over then pinch/press the shrimp to break the muscle fibers stretching the shrimp out as long as possible.

Stretching and breaking the fibers.

Before (on the right) and after.

The proportion of flour to egg/ice water mixture when making the *tempura* batter is about 1 to 1. Do not over mix the batter to prevent gluten fibers from forming which will toughen the batter making it less crispy. First dredge the ingredients in all purpose flour then dip them in the *tempura* batter. Now gently put them down into the oil. *Tempura* cooks quickly so watch carefully and always monitor the temperature of the oil.

Remove the cooked *tempura* and drain on a rack. Do not stack the pieces so all the steam is allowed to escape the interior of the cooked *tempura*.

When using *shiso* leaf or *nori* for *tempura*, dredge only one side in the flour and batter.

Keep the oil cleaned of stray batter to keep the oil fresh, preventing these little pieces of batter from burning and/or adhering to the other *tempura* pieces being fried.

*Somen* noodles can be used for a lovely decoration: wrap one end of a small bundle of dry *somen* noodles with a strip of *nori* (dampen *nori* so it will stick to itself). Drop the wrapped bundle of *soba* noodles into the hot frying oil then drizzle *tempura* batter over the noodles to achieve a flowering tree effect. This is used as a garnish and can be made ahead and kept for use when needed.

The shrimp is first dredged in flour then in the *tempura* batter. Gently slide the shrimp full length into the hot oil then drizzle more batter on the shrimp while frying to create a fluffy, crispy final product. Serve with the heated 4:1:1 sauce on the side with grated *daikon* and ginger mixed in. Four keys to good *tempura* are: Temperature, quality of the oil, mixing, and good flour.

*Age-dashi tofu*:
Press the water out of the *tofu* then dredge in flour, egg wash, and if desired, bonito flakes. Gently place in the hot oil. Use 4:1:1 dipping sauce with grated *daikon* and ginger.

*Yose-age*:
Julienne carrot, squash, potato, bay shrimp, green beans, etc. Dredge in flour then *tempura* batter.
Form into balls then deep fry.
Use 1:1:1 (*dashi*, *mirin*, soy) for dipping sauce.
Rather than using dipping sauce some alternatives are sea salt, ground mixed chili peppers or green tea powder with Hawaiian red sea salt.

Scallops:
Slice the scallops in half, dry, dredge in flour then the egg wash (beaten eggs) and finally in *panko*.
Or, to ensure the toppings stick, dredge in flour then in *tempura* batter and finally in a topping of *panko*, cornflakes, oatmeal, black sesame seeds, or crumbled *soba* noodles, etc.

Another attractive display item is to bundle dry *somen* noodles at each end with a strip of dampened *nori* then place the bundle in the frying oil. Force open the center of the bundle with the bottom of a ladle or chopsticks to create a canoe shape to fill as a container.

# Donburi

## Donburi

In general the primary ingredients are 4 *dashi* - 1 *mirin* 1 soy sauce mixture, green onion cut in a bias, thinly sliced yellow onion, and one beaten egg when using a Donburi pan. Donburi pan offers portion control (one serving), easy pour, and temperature control.

Equipments used for Donburi are measuring cup, ladle, and Donburi pan.

*Oyako-donburi* (*Oyako-don*): Page 19

*Katsu-don*: Page 25

*Tekka-don* (Tuna *donburi*):
Marinate tuna in soy sauce for one minute then arrange on steamed rice in a rice bowl. Spoon a mixture of *wasabi* paste and soy sauce over the top.
Sprinkle julienne of *nori* on the rice and serve with pickled ginger. Garnish with diced green onion.
To freeze fresh tuna, double wrap tightly in plastic wrap to eliminate any air. Keep frozen up to 10 days. Use for seared tuna, spicy tuna rolls or other similar dishes but not for *sushi* or *sashimi*.

*Una-don* (*Unagi donburi*):
Packaged eel (frozen barbecued eel) is used. Cut the package in half length wise to remove an eel filet. Cut in three pieces then grill them in a toaster oven. Serve on a bed of steamed rice in a rice bowl garnished with eel sauce and *sansho* or sesame seeds.
*Unagi* is oily, rich in Omega 5 oil and is an excellent summer time dish.

*Ten-don* (*Tempura* shrimp *donburi*):
Dredge the shrimp in flour then *tempura* batter. Gently lay the shrimp full length in the hot oil. When cooked, drain, then immediately dip the shrimp in heated 1:1:1 sauce.
Place on a bed of steamed rice in a bowl. Top with *tempura shiso* leaf then drizzle a little of the 1:1:1 sauce over the top.

# *Nabe*

## *Nabe* (One Pot Dishes):

*Negima Nabe* (Tuna onion pot):

Parboiled tuna pieces with spinach and green onions.

To cook the tuna onion dish pour a 7 parts *dashi* - 1 part sugar - 1 part light soy sauce mixture into the ceramic cooking pot (*donabe*). Add several slices of ginger then add the seared (parboiled) tuna, white ends of green onions, spinach, and napa cabbage. Cover the pot and simmer until the onions begin to soften.

Add the tops of the green onions simmering until soft; Serve. The ceramic pot (*donabe*) for cooking the tuna onion dish is pictured.

Tuna and mackerel are strong flavored fish so adding ginger or cooking with *daikon* draws out the strong fish flavor moderating and mellowing the taste.

*Zosui* is reheating steamed rice in the stock left in the pot.

## *Yakumi* (Condiments):

*Momiji-oroshi* (Grated *daikon* and red chili, or grated *daikon* mixed with chili paste):
After grating the *daikon* and red chili, squeeze out the excess moisture using a *makisu*.

*Ponzu* Sauce (Left on right picture):
  1 part *daidai* (citrus)
  1 part soy
  1 part vinegar
  1 part *mirin*
  1/2 part *tamari*
  *konbu* kelp (in the container)

*Ponzu* Sauce and Sesame paste sauce

Sesame paste sauce:
  5 Tbls sesame paste
  2 Tbls white *miso*
  2 Tbls *mirin*
  1 Tbls vinegar
  1/2 cup *dashi*
  1 Tbls sugar
  1 pinch minced garlic
  1 pinch grated ginger
  2 Tbls soy

More sugar can be added for sweetness if desired. Sesame paste substitutes are peanut butter or tahini butter.

*Sarashi-negi* (Chopped/rinsed green onions):
  Place the chopped green onions in a piece of cheese cloth; rinse under cold running water. Squeeze out the gooey liquid that forms. This process yields milder onions. Mix the above ingredients with *ponzu* sauce.
  (For more information see page 15)

*Shabu-Shabu* pan:

*Sukiyaki* pan:

## *Shabu-Shabu*:

*Shabu-Shabu* is cooked on the stove or at the table on a table-top stove in a convivial celebratory manner. Add water to the *shabu-shabu* pan with a piece of *konbu*, cover and bring to the boil. Add the tofu, cabbage rolls, cabbage, mushrooms, and green onions then simmer until the vegetables soften. Using chopsticks immerse a piece of the meat in the pot to cook. When the meat is cooked as desired, dip into the sauce and enjoy.

The dipping sauces used are *ponzu* with *momiji-oroshi* and *sarashi-negi*, or sesame paste sauce. (Page 39)

## *Sukiyaki*:

Heat 1-2 Tbls of oil in the *sukiyaki* pan over medium heat (on a portable table top stove if desired).

Sauté the noodles, beef, tofu, and the vegetables with 3 Tbls of sugar and 4 Tbls soy sauce. The vegetables will release water into the pot mixing with the sugar and soy sauce. Adjust the sauce in the pan by adding sugar and soy sauce to taste or by adding a little stock if more liquid is desired.

When preparing the vegetables for *shabu-shabu* and *sukiyaki* present them on a plate for cooking at the table. When boiling napa cabbage first immerse the white stem ends in the boiling water for 1 minute then immerse the greens with the stem ends.

On a *makisu* place boiled napa cabbage leaves then layer on spinach leaves (raw), julienne of raw carrots, then roll together. Finish by cutting the roll into bite sized pieces.

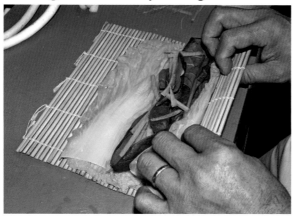

Slice uncooked cabbage, green onions, spinach, tofu, and yam noodles (in *sukiyaki*). Soy noodles are used in *shabu-shabu*. Also use small white mushrooms, small oyster mushrooms, shitake mushrooms cut in half with stems removed decorated with a star cut on the top, and carrot stars.

*Sukiyaki* is always beef where as *shabu-shabu* may be beef or pork.

*Sukiyaki* meat plate decoration:                    Pork for *shabu-shabu*:

## Fish

Use a gentle touch when handling fish to prevent bruising. Always support the fish with two hands. Fish is sensitive to 1 degree of temperature so remember when you are touching a fish with your hands at body temperature the fish is being cooked. Cooling your hands in ice water can be helpful when handling fish. Fish such as sardines, pompano, and squid are excellent quality at low price while yellowtail, salmon, and tuna are popular but expensive. Round fish include mackerel, salmon, tuna, yellowtail, etc. Flat fish include halibut and flounder. Triangular fish include eel, lingcod, and shark.

The *deba* knife is used to clean the fish. The first cut is just through the skin and flesh on the belly behind the pelvic fins. The second cut is from the top of the head down behind the pectoral fin to meet the first cut. Cut through the skin and flesh but not into the viscera. The third cut is a repeat of the second cut on the opposite side. Now grasp the head and tail bending the head upward separating the head from the body. The viscera will come out of the body with the head. (Page 77).

To filet the fish first cut only through the skin then cut through the flesh along the rib bones to the back bone both from the top of the fish along the dorsal fin and from the belly side of the fish. Now slide the knife under the loosened filet and separate it from the spine by cutting from the tail forward.

*Shimo-furi* or "hoarfrost" technique is to sear the skin by using boiling water. Pour boiling hot water over the skin then immediately immerse in ice water to prevent any further cooking. This is a popular technique used in preparing *tai* (sea bream). Oily fish such as tuna and mackerel are also treated in this fashion before simmering.

Fresh fish at the Los Angeles fish market.

## *Saba* (Mackerel):

*Shio-yaki* (Sea salt and grill):
Slice the filet into 3 pieces; cut an X just through the skin on each piece. Sprinkle with sea salt on both sides then grill 70% on the skin side and the remaining 30% on the flesh side of the filet.

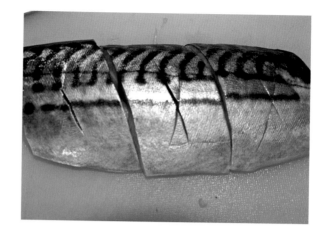

To finish:
Arrange the pieces on a plate with grated *daikon* and a *kikka daikon* flower;
Garnish with soy sauce.

*Saikyo-yaki*:
Use sea bass, cod, *saba*, etc.
200 grams white *miso* (for sweetness), 1/4 cup *mirin*, 1/4 cup *sake*, 1 Tbls light soy. Mix the ingredients together. Cut a filet into uniform size pieces then marinate in the *miso* mixture (overnight is best).
Grill the marinated fish 70% on skin side, 30% on flesh side. Finish with a darker sauce by adding dark soy sauce to a little of the marinade then simmer in a sauce pan for a few minutes. Arrange on a plate and serve the darkened sauce on the side or use a squeeze bottle to decorate.

# Saba

*Miso-ni*:

5 parts *sake* - 1 part *mirin* - 1 part light soy sauce - 1 part *miso*.

Cut saba filet into bite sized pieces; place on a metal tray skin side up, pour boiling water over the pieces then immerse in ice water. Remove the fish pieces draining off excess water.

Pour the *sake* and *mirin* into a sauce pan over medium heat; burn off the alcohol by igniting the fumes with a lighter or allowing the stove flame to ignite them. Burning off the alcohol using this method is called *nikiri*.

When the alcohol is burned off add the fish filet pieces to the sauce pan with slices of ginger; simmer covered with a circular paper vented to allow steam to escape.

Mix 1 to 1 *miso* and light soy sauce with a little of the liquid from the pan then add this mixture to the pan and cover with circular parchment or wax paper.

Serve in a shallow bowl.

Deep fried *Saba*:

Salt and pepper to taste, dredge in flour then in egg wash (beaten eggs), and finally in *panko*.

Fry in oil at 350°F until golden brown.

*Age-yaki* (Deep fried and grilled):
Marinate *Saba* filets in 60% *mirin* / 40% soy sauce mixture for 10 minutes; dredge in flour, deep fry 1 minute then set aside. In a frying pan sauté ginger and garlic then add the deep fried *Saba* filets; flash with 1/4 cup of *sake*, add the 60/40 *mirin*-soy mixture to the pan and reduce to caramelize. Remove the pan from the heat, add green onions, and serve.

*Age-Dashi* (*Tempura* deep fry using *Saba*):
Salt and pepper to taste, dredge in flour then egg wash. Deep fry at 350°F then remove from the oil and place in a sauce pan with 5:1:1 sauce (*dashi*, *mirin*, soy) and grated *daikon*. Bring to a gentle boil for one minute then place in a bowl and pour the 5:1:1 sauce over the top; garnish with green onion.

## Sashimi

*Sashimi* presentation and decoration is three dimensional having depth and height as well as area. Garnishes for *sashimi* plate decoration are called *Tsuma*. Knife technique is also important affecting the final appearance and presentation of the fish.

*Moritsuke* (Decoration):
There are three key elements in *sashimi* decoration: *Ten* (sky), *Chi* (ground), and *Jin* (human).
This three element concept is taken from traditional Japanese flower arranging. *Ten* (sky) and *Chi* (ground) are always in the same relationship on the plate while, as in life, *Jin* (the human element) is changeable. *Ten*, *Chi*, and *Jin* form a three dimensional triangular presentation on the plate.

There are four keys when considering *moritsuke* decoration: location, balance, color, and space in a 40/60 ratio. That is, 40% of the plate area is occupied by the *sashimi* while 60% of the plate area should remain empty.

On a long rectangular plate, the *Ten* (sky) *Chi* (ground) remain, as always, in the same relationship to each other while the *Jin* (human) area of the presentation is moved out to balance the space.
Creating *moritsuke* step by step:

*Daikon*, a large white radish, is integral to *sashimi* presentation. To prepare the *daikon* it is peeled around the circumference into a long continuous sheet (*Katsura-muki*) then chopped into julienne.

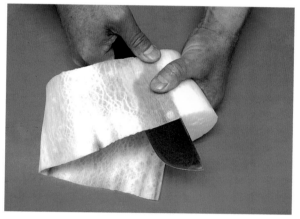 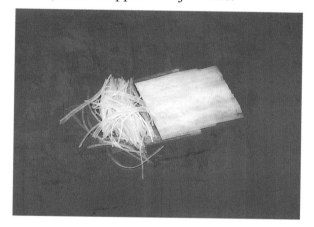

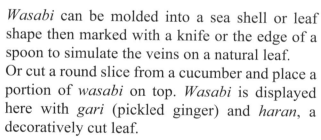

*Wasabi* can be molded into a sea shell or leaf shape then marked with a knife or the edge of a spoon to simulate the veins on a natural leaf.
Or cut a round slice from a cucumber and place a portion of *wasabi* on top. *Wasabi* is displayed here with *gari* (pickled ginger) and *haran*, a decoratively cut leaf.

*Tosa* shoyu (*Tosa* soy sauce):
This is the preferred dipping sauce for *sashimi*.

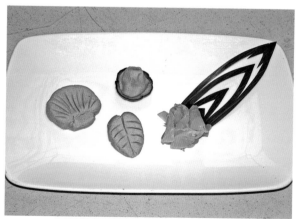

To prepare: Mix the *sake* and *mirin* then burn off the alcohol. Place all of the ingredients in a bowl; let stand 24 hours. Strain through cheese cloth and store in a cool dark place for 30 days. The best flavor comes after 6 months to 1 year and will keep 2-3 years. In an emergency, for a dipping sauce use dark soy sauce mixed to taste with mirin from which the alcohol has been burned off.

*Tosa* soy sauce:
    1 part - *sake*
    2 parts - *mirin*
    7 parts - dark soy sauce
    3 parts - *dashi*
    1/3 oz - *katsuo-bushi* (small hand full)

*Aji Tataki* (Spanish mackerel):
Scale the fish then cut off the exterior hard scale line on either side near the tail. For whole fish decoration, remove the gills and viscera together by cutting just behind the gills and back to the viscera cavity. Cut the gills loose behind the mouth and pull out the gills and viscera together. Keep the head on while filleting the fish. Remove the skin from the filet. Cut the filets into 3/8 inch cubes, add sea salt, finely grated ginger, and chopped green onions.

Arrange julienne *daikon* on a plate as a supporting bed for decorating the skeleton (bend the skeleton in a gentle curve; hold in place with a bamboo skewer).

Arrange *daikon* on the fish skeleton with a *shiso* leaf, place the diced filets on top of the *shiso* leaf. Garnish with lemon rind strips attached to lemon circles and carrot leaves. Serve with *ponzu* sauce on the side. When decorating the plate with a whole fish (*sugata-zukuri*) the head is to the left.

*Tsukuri sashimi*
- *Sugata-zukuri*: whole fish *Tsukuri*
- *Ike-zukuri*: live fish *Tsukuri*
- *Ike-jime*: bought live; then fish is killed at the fish market
- *No-jime*: the fish dies naturally

*Ike-zukuri*:
Live fish presentation is done by stunning a live fish then filleting one side of the fish leaving the fish otherwise intact. This is done within 2 minutes including making the *sashimi* from the filet as well as garnishing and decorating (make garnish and decorations ahead). The fish should be served with in 5 minutes of swimming in the aquarium.

*Saba neta* cutting:
Heavy salt marinate (*beta-jio*) for 2 hours rinse in water for 10 minutes. Marinate in 1:1 vinegar and water solution for 20 minutes.

Dry and wrap in wax paper and plastic wrap; place in the refrigerator to chill. (See page 86 for detailed *saba sushi* preparation)

Remember that fish is sensitive to 1 degree of temperature so be cautious when touching the flesh with your hands. Body warmth adversely affects the quality of the fish.

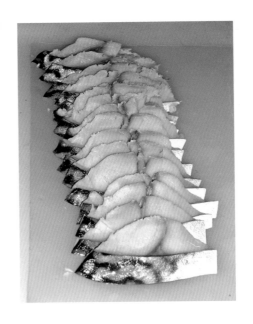

## New Style Sashimi

*Tai sashimi*:

Cut *neta* pieces (*neta* pieces are four fingers wide for the length and two fingers wide for the width) then lay radish sprouts across the pieces and roll them up inside. Sprinkle with salt and *ponzu*. Finish with *momiji-oroshi*.

*Tai* carpaccio:

The filet is first seared with scalding water on the skin side then immersed in ice water. Slice *neta* pieces from the filet then arrange them on a plate. Top with a pinch of sea salt, jalapeño-*masago*, julienne of ginger, a dab of Sriracha/honey sauce, and a cilantro leaf.

To serve cold, pour cold grape seed oil over the top then refrigerate for 5-10 minutes.

To serve hot, heat the grape seed oil before poring over the fish pieces then serve straight away.

*Hirame* hot oil carpaccio:

Thinly slice halibut garnishing with sea salt, green onion, julienne of ginger, a dash of chili paste, a squeeze of lemon, and a drop of *yuzu* (citrus).

Then sear with hot grape seed oil.

## *Hirame* (Halibut):

The head and eyes are to the left when the stomach is towards you with halibut, while the head and eyes are to the right when the stomach is towards you with flounder. Remove scales by slicing them off with a sharp knife; *hirame* flesh is fragile and is easily damaged by using a scaler.

Remove the head with a triangle cut around the head, chop through the spine then remove the head and viscera together.

 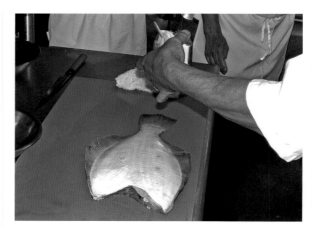

To filet: slice through the skin only at the 1-4 positions in the drawing - at the tail, along the fins, and at the centerline. Cut longitudinally down to the bone at the centerline then starting at the tail, cut off the filet by lifting and cutting down to the rib bones.

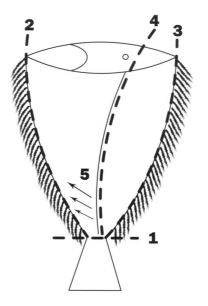

To remove the filets use a petty knife or other knife with a flexible blade to follow the contours of the skeleton when cutting the filet from the fish. Lift the filet gently as you go to facilitate cutting with accuracy and no damage. On the stomach side start the cutting at the tail end and slice towards the head; on the top side of the fish start the knife at the head end and cut towards the tail.

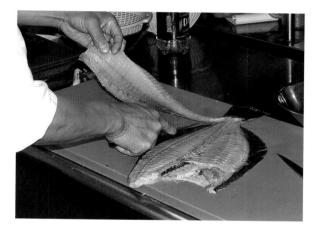

Trim the filet of bones, trim off the tasty flesh (called *engawa*) on the outer edge of the filet along the side fins, then remove the skin. When removing the skin from the filet keep the knife next to the skin to prevent waste. After filleting, never rinse the filets in water; use ice water only if necessary.

Wash the blood line out of the viscera cavity before cutting the filets from the bones. Rinsing the filets in water dilutes the delicate flavors of the fish. The skeleton can be cut at the second longitudinal bone for a deep fried appetizer.

Use the remainder of the skeleton for making stock.

The *nigiri* can be garnished with salt and lemon then seared with a hand torch; finish with *ponzu* sauce.

## *Sawara* (King Mackerel):

Clean and filet in the usual manner then *ogi-gushi* (skewer the filets fan style).

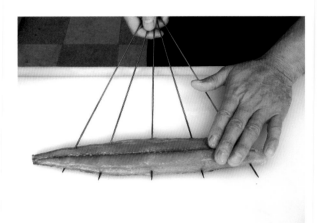

*Yaki-shimo* (sear the filet over a flame) on the flesh side first then on the skin side.
After searing immerse in ice water for 5 minutes and pat dry. Sear but do not cook.

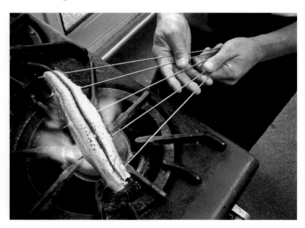

For nigiri sushi, place the filet skin side down with the tail toward you.
Cut at an angle with a slicing motion from the heel of the knife to the tip.

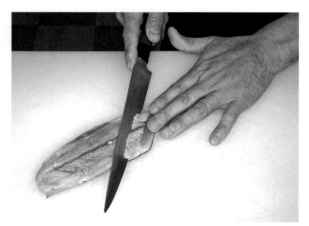

## *Ise-Ebi* (Lobster):

Have all the garnish and decoration ready ahead of time to decorate the plate before cutting the lobster. Insert toothpicks into two pieces of *daikon* to support the head and tail sections of the lobster on the plate. Cover the *daikon* supports with julienne *daikon* then place bamboo leaves over the *daikon*.

Cover the eyes with a towel then make the following incisions to sever the head and tail. Cut first on the top side of the lobster between the base of the head shell and the beginning of the tail shell. Then cut in the same place on the underside of the lobster to remove the whole head intact. Arrange the head on the plate then hold the tail section with the towel to make the cuts to remove the shell. After cutting along the sides and at the base of the tail insert your thumbs and gently remove the tail flesh then slice length wise down the center of the tail flesh. Immerse half in ice water then cut into bite sized pieces to serve. Shock the other half of the tail flesh in hot water for about 2 seconds followed with immersion in ice water; cut into bite sized pieces.

Add the tail shell to the head arrangement on the plate to serve the lobster. Arrange the pieces of tail flesh on the tail shell then garnish the plate with carrot leaves, cucumber fans, and lemon slices.

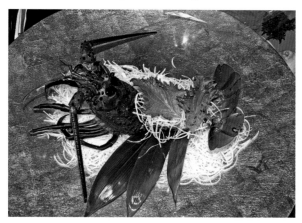

As mentioned, when serving lobster immerse the flesh in ice water only then serve, or sear for a second in hot water then immerse in ice water.

The tail flesh of the lobster may also be served 1/3 *sashimi*, 1/3 *tempura*, 1/3 stir fry; and finally, to finish, a *miso* soup using the head portion is made.

Split the head in half length wise down the center then place in water to simmer.

# Vegetable Cutting

Cut the cucumber length to exactly half the length of the nori sheet. Each cucumber yields 12 pieces by cutting in the following manner:

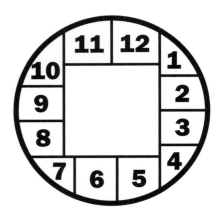
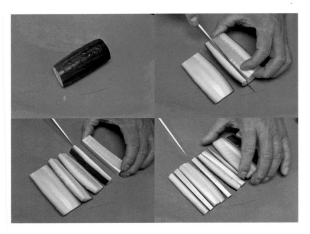

Avocados are cut into 16 to 24 pieces. For a California roll two pieces of avocado and two pieces of cucumber are used per roll so 1 avocado cut into 16 pieces will make 8 rolls while 1 cucumber will make 6 rolls. Therefore, to make 100 California rolls for example: 100 divided by 6 equals 16 + 1/3 cucumbers while 100 divided by 8 equals 12 + 1/2 avocados.

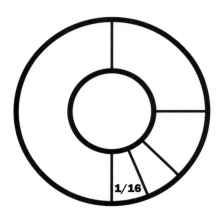
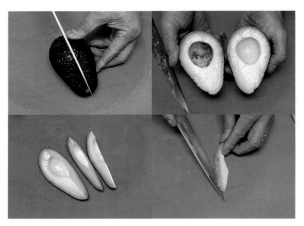
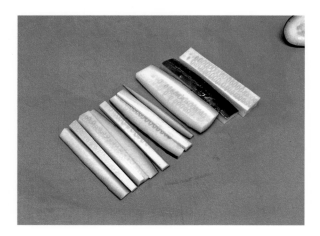

# Rice Preparation

Washing: 1-3 minutes.

Rinsing: more than 6 times.

Drying: 20-30 minutes minimum.

Cooking: 45 minutes.

Rice must dry before cooking so the moisture content inside and outside is equal insuring that water added for cooking is an accurate measurement.

New crop rice contains 15% moisture while old crop rice contains 12% moisture. The amount of water added for cooking the rice must be adjusted accordingly. Rice retains its moisture content from harvest (late October or November) for about four months. So by late March, the rice is considered Old Crop.

*Sushi* Rice:

Old Crop: 10 cups rice + 10 cups water.
New Crop: 10 cups rice + 9 1/2 cups water.

Steamed Rice:

Old Crop: 10 cups rice + 10 1/2 cups water.
New Crop: 10 cups rice + 10 cups water.

If rice is cooked in an electric rice cooker, any amount more than 5 cups, add 1 cup of water.

Rice dishes:

- *Sushi*
- *Onigiri* - Rice ball.
- *Zosui* - Left over Nabe stock with rice and egg.
- *Okayu* - Rice soup.
- *Takikomi* - Rice cooked simultaneously with other ingredients.
- *Ochazuke* - Rice in a bowl with green tea; often served late after celebrating.

## *Sushi* Rice

*Sushi* rice is served at 100°F so it is in the middle of the temperature danger zone of 41°-135°F.
It is permissible to keep the rice for 4 hours according to the Los Angeles health department regulations.
That is 2 hours to cool down to 100°F then from the moment that the rice is touched to be served, the rice
can be kept for 2 hours. If rice is to be kept longer, it must be tested and documented for Ph level.
It must be under 4.6 ph. This document record must be kept in the kitchen. So a useful rice cycle is to have
a batch of rice cooked at 11:00 am to last 4 hours until 3:00 pm which is through the lunchtime meal. Then
for the evening meal a batch of rice ready at 5:00 pm and another at 6:00 pm which is good until 9:00 pm
and 10:00 pm respectively.
One cup of dry rice equals 10 ounces of cooked rice which will make 2 rice outside rolls, 3 rice inside
rolls, or 8 *nigiri* pieces.

Sushi rice is made with medium/short-grain and
short-grain variety of rice.

 Long-grain rice (top),
 medium/short-grain rice (center),
 and short-grain rice (bottom).

*Sushi-zu* is often a well guarded secret among
*sushi* chefs as *sushi* rice is the chef's signature.
The formula is 7 vinegar - 5 sugar - 1.5 to 2 sea salt.
If using regular table salt the salt proportion is 1
part. This mixture is then aged with *konbu* kelp in
the storage container.
It is best to age *sushi-zu* for at least 2 weeks with
kelp to mellow and meld the flavors.
*Sushi-zu* will keep up to one year.

When making *Sushi* rice, add 15% *Sushi-zu* by
volume. So if cooking 10 cups of rice, add 1.5 or
1½ cups of *Sushi-zu*. For 5 cups of rice, add .75
or ¾ cups of *Sushi-zu*.

Mixing *sushi-zu* and the rice is done in a *hangiri* (wooden mixing tub) using a *miyajima* (mixing paddle). Always dampen the *hangiri* with water before putting the rice inside to prevent sticking. Pour the *sushi-zu* over the rice distributing evenly. Mix the rice and *sushi-zu* in about two minutes.

The *miyajima* is used in a rapid slicing motion to mix the *sushi-zu* into the rice. Spread the rice to a depth of about 2 inches and let cool for 5 minutes. Then flip the rice over and let cool for 5 more minutes. When removing rice from the *hangiri* hang a damp towel over the edge of the rice tub to prevent the rice from falling on to the edges and sticking there.

*Nori*, (dried seaweed processed into sheets for *sushi* rolls), is cut in half along the lines in the *nori*. The *nori* is used shiny side down, that is, the rice is layered on to the non-shiny side. The darker the color of the *nori* with a sea fragrance is the better quality. *Nori* ranges in price from 3 cents a sheet to 3 dollars a sheet. Usually 18-20 cents a sheet is good quality *nori* for *sushi* making. *Nori* should be crispy so it can be easily eaten. Toasting *nori* will make it crispy.

## *Maki Mono*

Making *maki mono*:
Rice inside rolls use 90 grams of rice distributed in 6 movements whereas rice outside rolls use 120 grams of rice distributed in the same 6 movements.

Make an oblong ball with the 90 grams of rice half the length of the *nori* sheet. Place the rice to the right side of the *nori* sheet and push with three fingers of the right hand towards the left while pulling and guiding the rice with the left hand.

The left hand is placed along the left edge to control the rice and keep it even with the edge of the *nori*. The 1st movement is to push and pinch rice at the upper left corner of the *nori*.

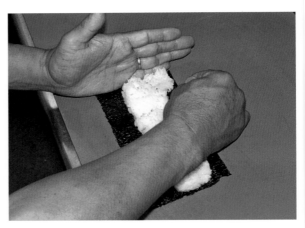

The 2nd movement is to pull the rice down to the lower edge along the left side using the fingers of the right hand.

Repeat these steps on the right side of the *nori* sheet for movements 3 and 4.

The 5th movement is pinching the rice at the top of the *nori* sheet with the fingers and thumbs of both hands.

The 6th movement is pulling the rice down to the lower edge of the *nori* using the fingers of both hands. Finally, sesame seeds are sprinkled on the rice.

Outside rolls use 120 grams of rice and cover the entire sheet of *nori*, (pictured above.) To make rice inside rolls, the top edge, about 10% of the *nori* sheet, is left uncovered with the rice. (See page 61).

*Goma*:

White sesame seeds must be toasted. To toast sesame seeds use a frying pan on medium to low heat and constantly move the seeds. The seeds should be ready when the aroma of sesame is present. Cool the seeds and place is a shaker with large enough holes. Already toasted sesame seeds can be purchased at Asian grocery stores.

*Temizu*:

*Temizu* is used to maintain moisture on hands while making sushi. Mix cold water with 5% rice vinegar (or less), to make the solution.

*Wasabi*:

To make *wasabi* from powder form, place the powder *wasabi* in a bowl and slowly drizzle water and mix until desired consistency. Desired consistency should be as soft as your earlobe. Store in an air tight container or place the container up side down to avoid *wasabi* paste from drying out.

*Kappa-maki* (Cucumber roll):
*Kappa* is from the traditional Japanese cartoon character's habit of eating cucumbers. Rice is on the inside with sesame seeds, *wasabi*, and cucumber. The cucumber roll illustrates the basic techniques for all roll making using the *makisu*. The *nori* is placed on the *makisu*. Rice is spread on the *nori* except the top 1/2 inch. A little *wasabi* is spread on the rice, sesame seeds are then sprinkled on the rice, and finally two slices of cucumber are laid end to end on the rice. Rice on the inside roll which use 90 grams of rice is pictured here.

The first movement is to fold the *makisu* up to ninety degrees.

The next movement is to roll the *makisu* over so the two edges of the rice meet, then pinch.

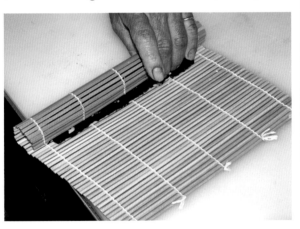

Roll the *makisu* one more time and pinch so the 1/2 inch of exposed *nori* meets the outside of the roll and sticks. The *kappa-maki* is ready to cut into pieces.

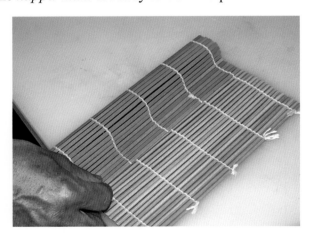

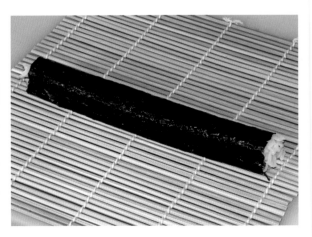

*Tekka-maki* (Tuna roll):

*Tekka* (casino) comes from the gambler's need to eat a little something without getting sticky fingers to hamper his gambling. So wrapping with *nori* became popular. Rice is on the inside with *wasabi* and tuna.

*Natto-maki* (fermented soy beans roll):

*Nori* outside; rice, *natto* mixed with soy sauce, hot mustard, (mix mustard powder with water) and *sarashi-negi* on the inside.

# Maki Mono: Shiso-Maki

To prepare a *shiso* leaf for *shiso-maki*, dampen the leaf a little then tuck it into the hollow made between the thumb and index finger of a closed fist. Pop the leaf by clapping the other hand over the top of it forcing air through. This will intensify the aroma and flavor.

*Shiso-maki*:
Rice inside roll with a prepared *shiso* leaf, a piece of pickled burdock, and plum sauce.

*Shiso-temaki* hand roll:
This is a small roll with just a little rice, a prepared *shiso* leaf, pickled burdock, and plum sauce. It is served at the end of a meal when the dinners are satiated to refresh the palate and fill up the last corner. Toast the *nori* over a flame. Roll horizontally in one hand.

Ingredients:
Plum sauce, *Yamagobo*, Cucumber, *Shiso* leaf

*Shiso-temaki* and *Shiso-maki*

California roll:

Rice with sesame seeds are on the outside with cucumber, avocado, and imitation crab stick on the inside. Fish cake can be combined with imitation crab stick 1-1 and mixed with mayonnaise to make crab mix for California rolls. For those who cannot eat imitation crab, fish cake is a good substitute. A mayonnaise, *mirin*, and soy sauce mixture is sometimes added to the crab recipe.

The *sushi* rice is spread on the *nori* covering the whole sheet, then sesame seeds are sprinkled over the rice. Flip the *nori* over then place fish cake or crab mix, cucumber, and avocado on the *nori*.

Form into a roll by hand. Cover with plastic wrap then place a *makisu* over the roll; press and form. Remove the plastic wrap then cut into pieces for presentation.

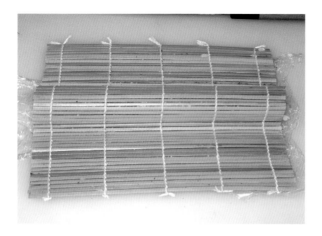

Special California roll:
Roll the long direction on the *nori* sheet with the rice and sesame seeds inside as well as avocado, cucumber, and crab stick. Cut into four pieces, arrange on a plate, top with julienne *daikon* and a *tempura shiso* leaf. Garnish with red and yellow sauces for contrast.

Caterpillar roll:
Julienne cucumber with heated eel is on the inside of the roll. Rice is on the outside with sesame seeds; a thinly sliced 1/2 of avocado is placed on top of the roll. Slice the avocado length wise. Peel one half then slice thinly across the width. Then press to the side creating a cascade effect.

Place the sliced avocado on top of the roll evenly distributing the slices along the length. Cover the roll with plastic wrap then press with a *makisu*.

Cut into bite sized pieces then repress the roll with the *makisu*.

When slicing, leave the end pieces larger to create a head and tail. Cut two small antennae from a jalapeño chili and two eyes using pickled burdock.

Garnish with eel sauce.

To make spicy tuna, dice tuna then mix with spicy tuna sauce: 65% mayonnaise, 30% sriracha or other red chili sauce, 5% sesame chili oil and ground red chilies.

Spicy tuna roll:
Avocado and spicy tuna mixture inside and rice outside with sesame seeds and jalapeño *masago*.

*Anago* eel and avocado roll:
Cucumber, avocado, and eel on the inside with rice and sesame seeds of the outside.

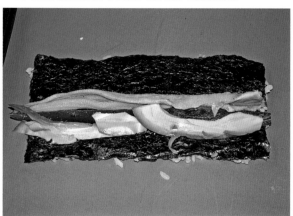

Volcano roll:
Make a special California roll as explained previously. Arrange on a plate and top with spicy tuna mixture. Add jalapeño *masago*, sriracha honey sauce, *wasabi* sauce, and *daikon* sprout. Decorate with mayonnaise, and two different colored sauces for contrast.

Rainbow roll:
Five types of fish slices alternated with a slice of avocado on the top of a California roll (or other kind of roll). Fish such as salmon, shrimp, yellow tail, halibut, mackerel, etc. may be used. Cover with plastic wrap and press with a *makisu*. Slice into bite sized pieces then repress. Garnish with *wasabi* sauce and sriracha/honey sauce.

# *Maki Mono: Special Rolls*

Shrimp crunchy roll:
Rice is on the outside with sesame seeds. Two *tempura* shrimp are inside with their tails extended out either end of the roll. Cover the roll with *tenkasu* (crunchy pieces of fried *tempura* batter or commonly known as *tempura* flakes), wrap with plastic wrap and press using a *makisu*. Slice into bite sized pieces then repress with the *makisu*.
Garnish with eel sauce and seaweed powder.

Shrimp crunchy roll special presentation uses julienne *daikon* as a foundation; six pieces of the crunchy roll are arranged on that, more *daikon* is then placed over the *sushi*. The two end pieces of the roll with the shrimp tails extended are placed on a second layer of *daikon*. Top with julienne green onion; garnished with butterfly cucumber slices. Finally, eel sauce and sweet red sauce are drizzled over the roll and three different colored sauces are used to decorate the plate.

Dragon roll:

Avocado and julienne cucumber on the inside with rice and sesame seeds on the outside of the roll. On top, three pieces of heated fresh water eel are laid on length wise allowing a tail to extend off one end. Cover with plastic wrap and press. Cut into bite sized pieces leaving the piece for the head larger than the other pieces. Serve on a long plate and garnish with *shiso* leaf split in half length wise for wings, horns and eyes are cut from pickled burdock, eel sauce is used for a garnish.

Spider roll:

Soft shell crab roll. Soft shell crab is frozen in different sizes and is available fresh in autumn.

Roll long direction with rice on the inside of the roll with julienne cucumber, avocado, *daikon* sprouts, *masago*, and deep fried soft shell crab. Dredge crab in flour only then deep fry. Cut the roll into six pieces and garnish with mustard sauce (2 mayonnaise - 1 mustard - a little honey), and sriracha/honey sauce.

Philadelphia roll:

Cream cheese, salmon (fresh or smoked), red onion, and capers are used. Cucumbers can be used as well or substituted for the capers. Roll and display in the flower style to resemble a bagel if desired.

# Maki Mono: Special Rolls

*Sawara* (King mackerel) special roll:
Mix chopped *shiso* leaf and *gari* (pickled ginger) with *sushi* rice. Spread the mixture on a sheet of *nori* for a rice outside roll. Inside, place julienne cucumber and avocado. Wrap *sawara* slices over the top of the roll then wrap with plastic wrap and press. Slice into bite sized pieces then garnish with grated ginger and jalapeño slices. Pour *ponzu* sauce over the top.

Salmon skin roll:
Rice and sesame seeds outside with bonito flakes. Salmon skin, cucumber, *daikon* sprouts, and *yama-gobo* (pickled burdock) are inside. Roll then finish with the bonito flakes (*katsuo-bushi*).

Peanut butter and celery roll:
Rice is on the outside with sesame seeds. Peanut butter and celery is rolled inside.

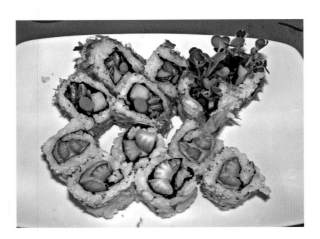

Special *maguro* roll:
Alternate slices of *Maguro* with a slice of avocado on the top of a California roll. Cover with plastic wrap then press with a *makisu*. Slice into bite sized pieces then repress. Garnish with wasabi sauce and sriracha/honey sauce.
Decorate the plate with eel sauce.

Barracuda roll:
Cucumber, avocado, and *Shiso* on the inside; rice on the outside topped with *neta* slices of barracuda garnished with *sansho* (Japanese pepper), and covered with *terakobu* (pickled seaweed).

*Hirame tempura* roll:
Use thinly sliced tail area pieces of the filet; arrange them on a sheet of *nori* to roll the long direction with avocado and *sarashi-negi*. Dredge the roll in *tempura* flour and batter followed by deep frying. Arrange on a plate garnishing with *ponzu* sauce, *wasabi*/mayonnaise sauce, and sriracha/honey sauce.

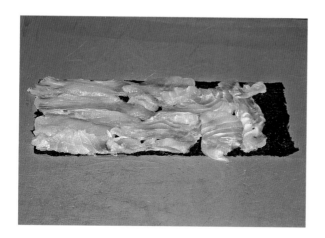 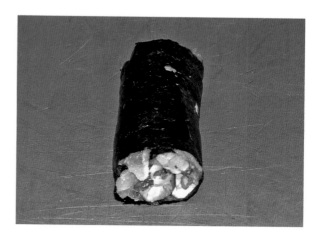

Cucumber special roll:
Peel a cucumber around the circumference to get a long skin (like a sheet of *nori*). On the cucumber skin place a *shiso* leaf, small amount of *sushi* rice, julienne *daikon*, julienne cucumber, *yamagobo*, *masago*, imitation crab stick, *daikon* sprouts, and some slices of tuna then roll all the ingredients in the cucumber skin. Use the outer peel of the cucumber and the center seed column left after peeling for garnish and decoration.

# Maki Mono: Special Rolls

*Daimyo* mega roll:

Glue two full sheets of *nori* together by lightly dampening one edge. Cover the *nori* sheets with rice except for the top one inch or so. In a thin egg sheet roll *ebi*, *unagi*, and *shitake* mushrooms then lay the egg roll on the rice. Now add cucumber, *inari* with sweet rice, *maguro*, *shake*, crab stick, *shiso*, avocado, *masago*, julienne carrot and *daikon*.

Roll all the ingredients inside the *nori* sheets.

*Shikai-maki*:

Rice mixed with dried pickled *shiso* leaf. Rice mixed with seaweed powder or rice mixed with orange and green *masago*. The idea here is to have different color rice to contrast in the final *sushi* roll. For the center of the roll stack rectangular cube cut cucumber and tuna with *tamago* or crab stick and wrap in *nori*. Cut *nori* sheets as follows: One full sheet is cut to yield one piece 60% of its length the other piece 40%.

In the 40% sheet of *nori* roll the colored rice. On the 60% sheet of *nori* spread white rice then wrap the 40% colored rice roll inside the 60% white rice *nori* sheet. In a full sheet of *nori* spread the other colored rice and roll the 40%/60% roll inside that. Now glue a full sheet to a sheet 30% of full length using a little water and sticky rice as glue.

Cut the full sheet three component roll in half length wise and each half in half length wise again to have four long quarter sections. Now place two of the quarters in the 30% *nori* sheet, the cubed four part center roll on that, and the other 2 quarter parts on top of that then roll all together. Press using a makisu then cut into sections for display.

*Temaki* (Hand roll):

Lay a sheet of *nori* on the palm of your left hand. Place the rice at a slight angle on the left side of the *nori* sheet. Make an indentation in the rice to receive the other ingredients. In this case, cucumber, avocado, and a crab stick. Fold the lower left corner of the *nori* sheet over the rice and other ingredients at a 45 degree angle. Using the right hand, wrap the right side of the *nori* sheet over the fold you have made and roll one revolution to the right.

# Gunkan Sushi

*Gunkan sushi*:
A 1 oz *nigiri* shape *sushi* rice wrapped with a piece of *nori* then filled with various loose ingredients which do not hold on top of *nigiri sushi*.
Cut *nori* for *gunkan sushi* as shown.
Cut two strips across the *nori* at one end of a half sheet for *hachimaki* (*Nigiri* bandana) then cut the remainder into 3 equal strips to wrap around the rice.

Wrap the rice with *nori* (adhering rice to textured/bumpy side) starting from the center.

Press down on the rice to make room for toppings. *Gunkan* presented with *masago* and *tobiko* on right.

*Saba Bo-sushi*:

Before the advent of *sushi* rolls wrapped in *nori*, a filet of *saba* or *sawara* was used. Butterfly the filet length wise laying the filet open. Use *wasabi*, *shiso* leaves, and rice on the inside. Roll in a damp piece of cheese cloth being sure to pack in the ends and roll tightly. Top with *terakobu* the pickled seaweed.

*Inari sushi*:

A packaged deep fried *tofu*. In a mixing bowl place rice, white and black sesame seeds and juice from the packaged *tofu* and mix well. Open the *tofu* piece and put 1 oz of rice in the pocket. Press down with the index finger, roll one side closed over the rice then the other side over that to form a seam covering the rice. Place seam side down when serving. Or use the *inari tofu* to emulate *gunkan sushi*. Pictured on the left is *inari sushi* with *tsutsumi sushi*, a wrapping technique. On the right *inari sushi* with julienne egg sheet, *ebi*, and a cucumber fan as garnish.

## *Sushi* plate arrangement

*Sushi* is arranged on the plate in either 4 way decoration - NEWS - north, east, west, south so the plate can be viewed from all directions, or 3 way decoration for 3 direction viewing, 2 way decoration for viewing from 2 directions or 1 way decorations for viewing the presentation from 1 direction. One way decorations include: *Sansui* - *San* (mountain) and *Sui* (water), is a representation of water running down hill. *Kikusui* is a representation of a chrysanthemum. One way decorations are traditionally arranged toward the right hand as in arranging *sashimi*.

A four way presentation.

A three way presentation.

A one way presentation.

A full table presentation.

# Fish

For freshness check color, feel for firmness (especially in the stomach area), there should be no damage on the body, the eyes should be fresh and clear, the gills red and free of mucous, and there should be no fishy odors.

Fish Directions:
*Kami* - forward toward head,
*Shimo* - back half towards tail;
*Se* is the upper half while *Hara* is the lower half.

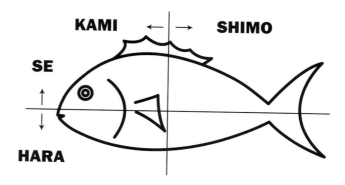

Again, *Shizuo Tsuji*, from the same source, tells us that, "Freshness, vividness of fish is essential to *sashimi*. Winter months are best for savoring *Hon-Maguro* (fatty tuna), *Sawara* (king mackerel), and *Shirauo* (tiny whitebait). April through June is *Tai* (sea bream or red snapper) as well as *Karei* (flounder). *Tai* is associated with cherry blossom time. Bonito is best in spring. Shrimp is best in the first days of summer. High summer is freshwater fish like carp, perch, and *unagi* eel. Autumn comes with mackerel, various bream, clams, and when cold sets in oysters and *hirame*."

*Yaki-shimo*:
Searing with fire. Use metal skewers fanned out at angles (*ogi-gushi*) through the filet so they can be grasped with one hand. The skewers should be inserted just above the skin. Salt the filet, sear, then immerse in ice water for 5 minutes. Remove and pat dry in a clean towel. Wrap in waxed paper and plastic wrap then refrigerate.

*Shikomi*: Preparing fish to the point it is ready for *sushi* or *sashimi*.

## *Tai* (Sea Bream / Red Snapper):

Sea Bream (Red Snapper) is associated with springtime and cherry blossom season. *Tai* yields much to Japanese cuisine with the head, bones, eggs, skin, flesh, liver, and parts of the intestine all being used. To scale place the fish inside a plastic bag to catch the scales.

 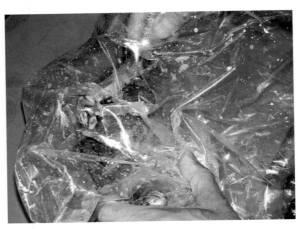

Severe the head using the 3 cut method then grasp the head and tail to remove the head with the viscera. (Be sure to grab the tail to prevent damaging the flesh).

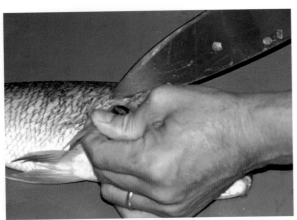 

Remove the filets using the 3 piece method. First cut just through the skin, then down to the spine along the rib bones.

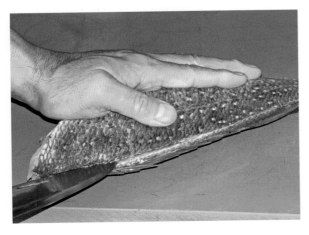 

Repeat this procedure on the belly side of the fish to remove the filet.

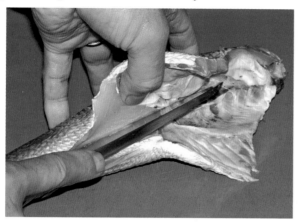

Remove the stomach bones by cutting near the spine then use a shallow scooping cut to remove the bones. Remove the center line bones by cutting along each side of the bones yielding 2 pieces from each filet.

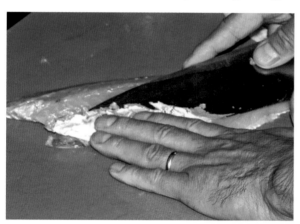

The filets are seared with hot water (*shimo-furi*) on the skin side only. Place the filets skin side up on a metal tray, cover with a paper towel, then pour the hot water over the paper towel and filet. Take care not to over saturate the filet with hot water; we do not want to cook the flesh. Then immediately immerse the filet in ice water.

An alternative treatment for the filets: skewer them using the *ogi-gushi* technique then sear them over a flame (*yaki-shimo*). Immerse in ice water immediately after searing.

Cut neta pieces from the filets.

Form *nigiri* sushi with the *neta* pieces; serve with a little sea salt and lemon juice or serve as *sashimi*. *Tai* and *Hirame*, like many white fish, use *ponzu* sauce, as well as *momiji-oroshi* and *sarashi-negi* as a garnish as well.

Split the head down the middle by setting the head on a cutting board with the mouth facing up. Insert the tip of a *deba* knife in the mouth then cut downward through the top of the head. Fold the head open to cut out the gills then slice the two sections apart.

Place the head pieces skin side up on a metal tray and sear with hot water (*shimo-furi*) which will loosen the scales. Remove the scales with the edge of a spoon then rinse in cold water.

 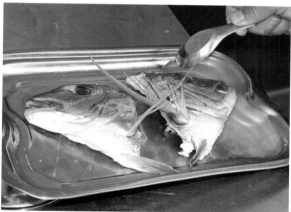

The head can be used in soups or simmered in a 5 *sake* - 1 *mirin* (*nikiri*) and 1 soy sauce. Cover with a wooden lid or cooking paper that fits inside the pan; simmer in the *sake* - *mirin* and a little bit of sliced ginger until the liquid is gone or nearly gone then finish with the light soy sauce.

*Tai* skin can be used to create an appetizer. After removing the skin from the filet shock in boiling water for 2 seconds then chop into small pieces. Mix with *ponzu* sauce then garnish with *momiji-oroshi* and *sarashi-negi*.

## *Shake* (Salmon):

Remove head and viscera in the usual way. Save the head for stock, the collar for grilling. Cut the filets from the skeleton and pull the bones out of the filets using a *hone-nuki* (bone pick), special tweezers for pulling bones. Measure 4 finger widths three times from the front of the filet toward the tail then cut the filet there.

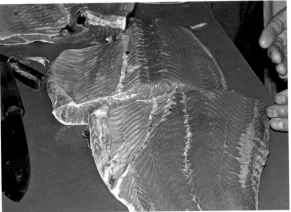

Immerse the filet in a 5% salt water solution for 1 hour (*Tate-jio* marination). Then rinse in fresh water. Another method is *beta-jio* (heavy salt) marination shown on right.

Salt the bottom of pan, then place the filet skin side down on the salt. Cover the flesh side with generous amount of salt, and let rest for 2 hours. Next rinse filet throughly in water 10-15 minutes.

After marinating, the salmon must be frozen for 1 week. Double wrap with plastic wrap before freezing to eliminate any air from the package. Before serving, defrost the salmon and marinate in 1/2 and 1/2 vinegar water solution for 20 minutes. Cut *neta* pieces to form *nigiri* or *sashimi*.

*Shake tsutsumi-sushi* garnished with *tobiko*.

*Shake*, *tai*, and *maguro sashimi*.

The salmon skeleton:
Scrape the flesh off the bones using the edge of a metal spoon. Use the bones in soup stock. Mince the flesh using a *deba* knife, add grated ginger, one beaten egg, salt, pepper, and *panko*, then mix all the ingredients together. Let rest for 10-15 minutes.
Make into balls and poach them in water. The salmon balls are a delicious addition to *miso* soup.

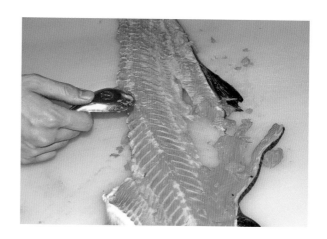

The head:
*Nashi-wari* is to cut the head longitudinally through the top. Remove the gills, cut off the collars (*kama*) to grill or use in soup stock.
Slice off the cartilage at the top of the head to marinate in vinegar and eat as a separate morsel.

## *Ika* (Squid):

Remove the head and viscera together by inserting your fingers into the body of the squid to separate them. Save the transparent endo-skeleton for garnish if desired. Cut the tentacles off just above the eyes, squeeze the top of the tentacles to force the mouth out then sever.

 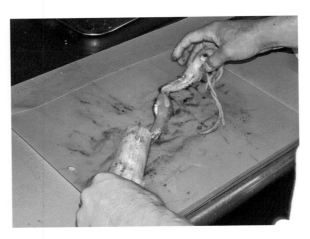

Cut off the ends of the longest tentacles. Pull the skin off of the body. Slice the body open along the "seam." Parboil the squid for about 15 seconds then immerse in ice water.

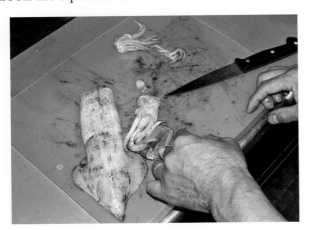 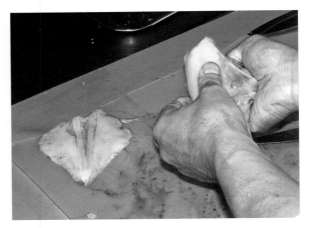

*Ika sushi*:

Clean and slice the body open. Cut a *neta* piece from the body flesh. *Neta* pieces are four fingers wide for the length and two fingers wide for the width.

Score the skin side with a cross hatch pattern. Immerse in boiling water for 30 seconds followed by immersion in ice water.

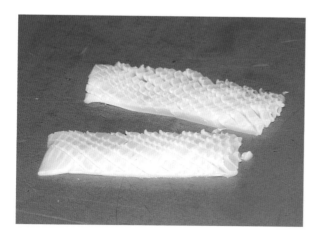

Julienne one piece of the squid body to make *nigiri*, then lay a *shiso* leaf on the rice ball, the julienne squid on the *shiso*. Garnish with lemon and sea salt.

The tentacles are split in half then immersed in boiling water for 15 seconds followed by ice water.

Sear the tentacles with a hand torch or over a flame with a little salt 20-30 seconds. Cut *nori hachimaki* (a tie strip of *nori*). *Hachimaki* means 8 rotations like the headband worn by *sushi* chefs. Wrap the tentacle piece of *nigiri* with a

*hachimaki* strip of *nori* then garnish with grated ginger and soy sauce.

The fin sections of the squid are split in half, seared in hot water, and then immersed in ice water.

Wrap the *nigiri* pieces with 1/2 of a *shiso* leaf *hachimaki* (rather than *nori*) then garnish with eel sauce.

# Ika

*Inro sushi* (Stuffed squid):

Leave the body of the squid whole.

Mince the parboiled tentacles and fin pieces (the fin pieces can be kept for *nigiri sushi*), add the minced tentacles to pickled ginger, shiso, pickled burdock, green onion, sesame seeds, rice, and eel sauce; mix well. Stuff the body of the squid with the rice mixture.

Pan Fry the stuffed squid briefly in grape seed oil adding a little soy sauce at the last minute. Slice then garnish with eel sauce and seaweed powder.

Squid *sashimi*:

Julienne cucumber, julienne the squid body.

Arrange the cucumber on a long plate; drape the squid over the cucumber and sprinkle sesame seeds on the squid, then julienne *shiso* leaf and jalapeño *masago*.

Now sear using hot grape seed oil then garnish with soy sauce and sear again with a flame torch.

Always select squid with a firm body that is fresh looking, glossy and free of mucous, without a fishy odor.

## *Saba* (Mackerel):

Clean and filet using 3 cut method, but do not remove rib bones around the belly area.

Marinate *Saba* filet for 2 hours in beta-jio (heavy salt marinade) then wash for a minimum of 10 minutes in cool water, then 20 minutes in 1:1 vinegar/water marinade.

Gently pat dry, first wrap in waxed paper then plastic wrap and refrigerate overnight before use.

For *sushi* Preparation remove center bones, rib bones and skin.

*Saba* is salted to keep good flavor and to counter any disagreeable odors. *Saba* can be *yaki-shimo* (Seared by fire) with salt and pepper or salt alone. As mackerel ages it becomes oilier. Searing adds interest and improves flavor.

*Saba nigiri* is garnished with grated ginger, green onions, and *ponzu* sauce.

# Nigiri

## Nigiri Sushi

Joining the *neta* piece and sushi rice ball to form. *Nigiri* is done in eight steps:
Place the rice ball centered on the *neta* piece;

1. Pinch the narrow sides using thumb and index finger.

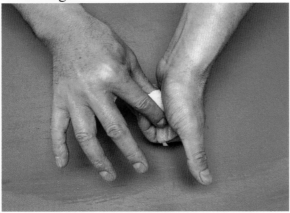

2. Press the top gently using index finger.

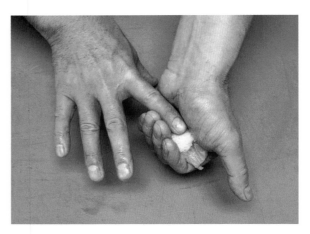

3. Roll the nigiri sushi a 180 degrees so that the fish is on top.

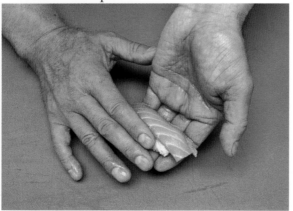

4. Pinch the sides and slide thumb over the top.

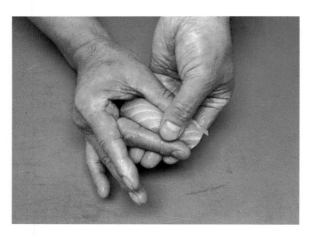

5. Gently press and shape.

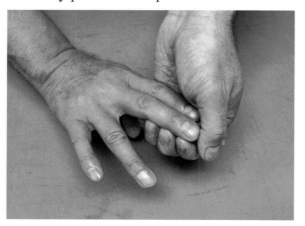

6. Turn end to end.

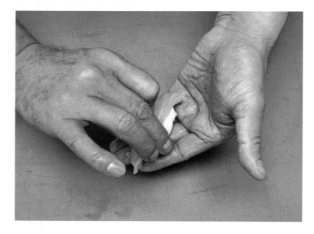

7. Gently press and shape. (Same as No. 5)

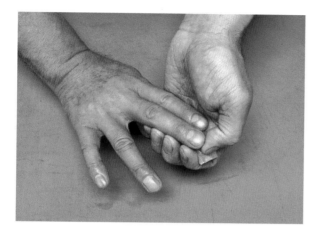

8. Pinch the sides and slide thumb over the top. (Same as No. 4)

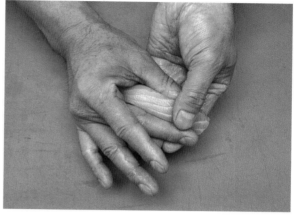

*Shake* (salmon) and *maguro* (tuna) *nigiri*.

Unagi (eel) *nigiri* with *hachimaki*.

*Nigiri* and Gunkan combination plate.

Vegetable *nigiri*.

## *Maguro* (Tuna):

Tuna identification: There are four types of Tuna commonly used in making *sushi* and *sashimi*:
Blue Fin, Big Eye, Yellow Fin, and Albacore.
Blue fin contains *Toro*, the delicious belly meat so prized by *sashimi* aficionados, and has dark red flesh with oily fat. Big Eye has bright red flesh and is also oily but less so than Blue Fin. Yellow Fin has bright glossy red flesh containing no fat or oils. Albacore has a brownish to red flesh with fatty oils and should be used immediately as Albacore sours quickly.

Selecting the best tuna starts here at the fish market.

Recognizing tuna filets:
1: This area is from the middle of the fish and contains little or no fiber; this is the best part of the filet.
2: This area is near the skin.
3: This area is near the tail containing the maximum amount of fibers.
4: This pattern indicates veins and blood line. Flesh from areas 2 and 3 are pictured on the right.

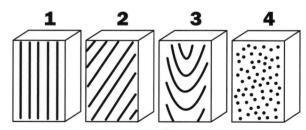

This piece is Big Eye tuna because the color of the flesh is changing from bright red to lighter red due to the fat content. Only Big Eye and Blue Fin change color in this way. Blue Fin is much darker red and has more fat content. The dark skin on this piece indicates that this piece comes from the upper part of the fish rather than the belly sections which have light to whitish skin.

To freeze tuna double wrap in plastic wrap. Vacuum wrapped is the best choice allowing the tuna to keep up to a week in the freezer. To defrost frozen tuna let stand for 20-30 minutes in 5% saltwater solution (*tate-jio*). Use immediately as tuna deteriorates rapidly after freezing. Tuna sours, so it must be used as quickly as possible. Remove the blood line immediately after purchase to prevent the blood from leaking into the adjoining flesh. Cut away any damaged or discolored flesh. Remove the skin, then wrap the filet in paper towels then double wrap in plastic wrap and refrigerate. The blood line leaking into adjoining flesh is an indicator of age and quality.

Bright red going to purple indicates that the quality is still improving. Bright red going toward brownish red indicates that the quality is deteriorating. *Sashi* is a tumor or blemish in the flesh of the tuna.

To use tuna blood line it must be soaked first in fresh water for several minutes then dredged in sauce. The sauce is ketchup, sriracha, sugar, sesame chili oil, pepper, salt, and soy.
Grill or pan fry briefly in butter. This makes a tasty appetizer.

# Maguro

*Sakudori*:

Tuna cutting in preparation for use in *sushi* and *sashimi*. Cut the filet to length which is 3 x 4 finger widths long. The tuna filet is then cut 3 fingers high and then in 1 thumb width sections for *neta* cutting. The pieces containing fiber can be grilled or seared in a frying pan with butter. The flesh can be scraped from the fiber for use in spicy tuna rolls. The grilled or seared pieces can be made into *sushi*. Make *nigiri* and serve with soy sauce and grated ginger. For show, squeeze a lemon or lime wedge on the edge of your knife and allow the juice to drip down the knife onto the *nigiri*.

*Neta* Cutting:

Each piece must be the same size. All types of fish must also be cut so the *neta* pieces are the same size and the finished *nigiri* looks similar. Cut with the skin side down, tail toward you, each piece is 2 finger widths wide and 4 finger widths long which is 1/2 ounce of fish. The *sushi* rice should be centered on the *neta* piece.

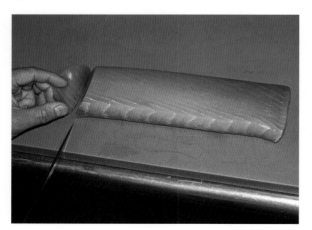 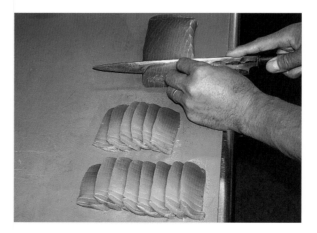

Farm raised Blue fin tuna can have a strong flavor and be very oily with a sour taste finishing with a distinct fishy tuna taste. The sour, oily taste and feel lingers on the teeth. To soften the flavor sear with a hand torch then use grated ginger and sea salt on top of the *nigiri* then squeeze a little lemon on the *nigiri*. This cuts the sour flavor adding an agreeable touch of citrus/lemon taste. The oily taste and oily feel on the teeth is eliminated as well. Garnish with soy sauce and *sarashi-negi*.

Tuna *shimo-furi*:

*Shimo-furi* is to sear with hot water. Immerse the tuna in steaming hot water for 30 seconds then immediately immerse in ice water for 30 seconds. Tuna can also be wrapped in a nori sheet and sliced.

Tuna can be "speared," that is, a slice is made in the center of a piece of tuna and cucumber is inserted inside. Tuna can be rolled in a sheet of daikon or be cut into 3/8 inch cubes then rolled in grated *daikon* and garnished with green onions. Another way is to slice the tuna thinly then lay the slices on a sheet of *nori*; place julienne of cucumber on the tuna and roll into *sushi* Roll.

# *Maguro: Toro*

*Toro* (Fatty tuna belly):
Pictured is delicious wild Blue fin *toro*. The piece is first *sakudori* cut; those pieces that will not be used immediately are double wrapped in plastic wrap then frozen for use within a few days.
*Toro* is quite oily deteriorating rapidly.

*Neta* pieces are cut, *nigiri sushi* is made, a pinch of salt is added, and then searing is done with a hand torch.

The *nigiri* in this case is finished with soy sauce and *sarashi-negi*. *Toro* pieces with fiber are seared in grape seed oil in a hot frying pan for 5 seconds on each side then *nigiri sushi* is made. The *nigiri* is then seared using a hand torch then garnished with grated ginger and a dash of soy sauce. *Toro* for *sashimi* can be cut from between the fibers.

Pictured here is *toro* tartar.

Mince the *toro* flesh then press into a mold; refrigerate to chill. Place in a bowl removing the mold. Top with *tobiko*, thin slices from the bulb end of a green onion, and thin slices of avocado forming a small fan.

Garnish with a lemon half-round.

The sauce is dark soy, *wasabi*, *yuzu*, and *yuzu* pepper. Serve with bread or crackers.

*Zuke* is tuna marinated in soy sauce; 1 *sake* - 1 *mirin* (*nikiri*) - 3 soy sauce. Burn the alcohol off the *sake* and *mirin* then add the soy sauce, mix well, and allow cooling. Pour into a tray long enough to accommodate a *sakudori* cut tuna filet. Roll the tuna in the marinade then cover with a paper towel saturated with the marinade mixture. Refrigerate for 1 hour. The tuna can also be seared *shimo-furi* (hot water) before marinating which changes the texture allowing the tuna to absorb more of the marinade flavor.

To serve, first skewer the tuna *ogi-gushi* style (fan shape) then sear over a flame (*yaki-shimo*).

Cut *neta* slices from the tuna then arrange them on a plate over julienne cabbage, cucumber, *daikon*, or a combination of these. Top with *miso* dressing then drizzle mayonnaise and sriracha/honey sauce over that; garnish with *sarashi-negi*.

## *Bincho Maguro* (Albacore):

Cut the albacore loin length wise into manageable pieces for neta cutting then skewer, salt, and sear over a flame (*yaki-shimo*). Black pepper can also be used when searing.

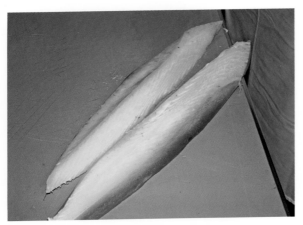
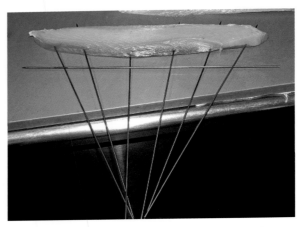

After searing immerse in ice water. Garnish by searing again with the hand torch, then top with ginger and *sarashi-negi* (rinsed green onion) and finish with *ponzu* sauce. A piece of *shiso* leaf placed between the *neta* and the rice ball is a delicious addition.

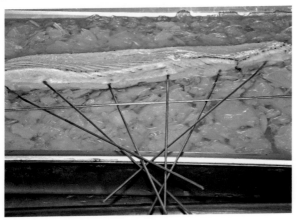

# Small Fish

Some small fish include:
- *Aji*: Spanish mackerel
- *Ebo-dai*: Pompano
- *Iwashi*: Sardine
- *Nishin*: Herring

Remember, fish are sensitive to 1 degree of temperature. Room temperature and body temperature cooks the fish, especially small fish. Keep them cold.

## *Aji* (Spanish Mackerel):

*Aji* is filleted using the three piece method (two filets and the skeleton). Marinate for 20 minutes in *furi-jio* (sprinkle salt marinade) then rinse in fresh water, and finally immerse 1:1 vinegar/water marinade for 2 minutes. Remove the bones and skin from the filets. Cut *neta* pieces in the usual fashion, skin side down tail towards you.

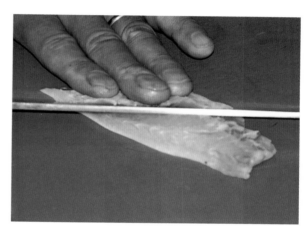

Make *nigiri sushi* garnished with grated ginger, *sarashi-negi*, and *ponzu* sauce.

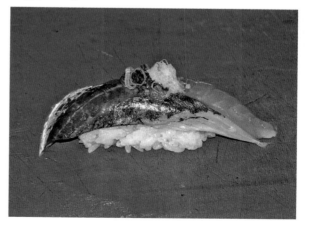

## *Ebo-dai* (Pompano):

Clean the fish as a small round fish.

The head is removed in one cut. Remove the viscera using the index finger. Filet in the usual manner using the 3 piece method. Marinate the filets in *tate-jio* (5% saltwater marinade) for 20 minutes then rinse in fresh water and then immerse in 1:1 vinegar/water solution for 2 minutes.

Pompano *sushi*:

After a light vinegar marinade of 1-2 minutes peel the skin off the filet, cut out the middle boney section. Now there are four pieces - 2 from each filet.

Slice partially through the filet length wise to butterfly each piece open to make a *neta* piece for *nigiri sushi*.

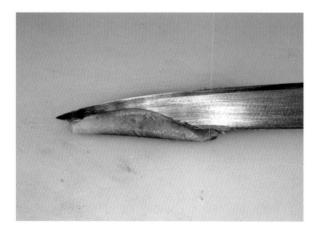

Or pull the bones out of the filet using a *hone-nuki* (special tweezers).

The skeleton can be hung near the stove to dry then deep fried two times for a crispy snack. Drain excess oil and allow drying between frying.

## Vinegar Solution

To marinate fish filets in the vinegar solution, mix 1 part rice vinegar with 1 part cold water. Refrigerate the vinegar solution to insure coldest temperature possible before marinating the filets.

## *Iwashi* (Sardine):

Clean off any scales, remove the head in one cut then cut off the lower part of the belly in one straight cut. Clean out the viscera then insert the thumbs into the fish stripping the flesh off of the bones by sliding the thumbs from the center in opposing directions along the spine.

Deep fry the skeleton, serve with salt for a delicious snack.

The filets must be lightly salted (*furi-jio*) for 15 minutes then rinsed in fresh water, and then immersed in a 1:1 vinegar/water solution for 2 minutes. Cut out the fine bones at the center line and edges of the filets. Two filets yield four *neta* pieces. Remove the skin then lightly slice the flesh underneath in a cross hatch design.

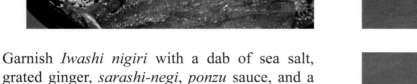

Garnish *Iwashi nigiri* with a dab of sea salt, grated ginger, *sarashi-negi*, *ponzu* sauce, and a little soy sauce.

*Iwashi* stays fresh only 1 day so prepare fish in the morning to be eaten at noon or not later than the evening meal.

## *Nishin* (Herring):

Herring is filleted by removing the body from the skeleton in one piece. To cut *neta* pieces slice the tail as well as the dorsal fin and bones from the filets. Remove the skin then make two length wise cuts in a filet leaving them connected at one end. Braid the three strands of the filet together to form a *nigiri* piece. Another option is to make shallow diagonal slices in the skin side of the filet then roll the filet skin side out, cut through the center of the roll leaving a hinge to butterfly open. See below.

Or after making the shallow diagonal cuts use the filet as is to form a *nigiri sushi* piece.

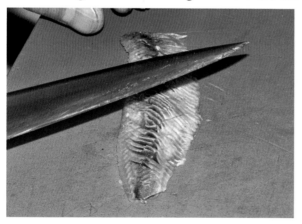

## *Anago* (Sea Eel):

Remove the head and slice off the dorsal fin and the belly fin. De-bone then lay the eel on a flat surface and pour hot water (*shimo-furi*) on the skin side of the filet. Scrape off the skin using the edge of a metal spoon then rinse in fresh water.

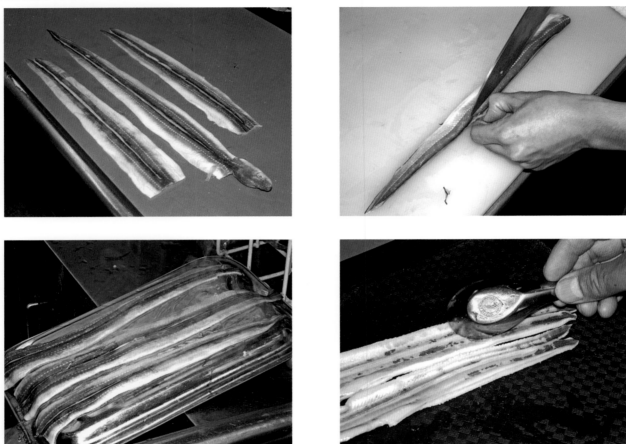

To make the eel sauce:

Simmer the heads in fresh water for stock. Then simmer the eels for 45 minutes in 3.5 cups *sake* (*nikiri* - burn off alcohol),  7.5 cups eel stock (strained) from simmering the heads, 10 ounces of sugar, and 6 ounces of light soy sauce. Cover the eels when simmering with waxed paper.

Set the eels aside after simmering and reduce the stock by 70%. The reduction is correct when the sauce is covered with small bubbles. Measure the volume of what is left after the reduction then add 1/3 that amount of soy sauce, 1/3 sugar, 1/3 tamari, and a pinch of sea salt.

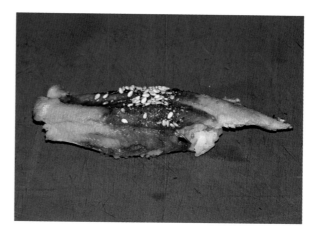

Test the thickness of the sauce by running a bead of the sauce on a long plate then tipping the plate vertically to observe the viscosity. The sauce should "hang" on the plate rather than run off. Continue reducing the sauce until the desired thickness is achieved. The sauce can be "seeded" (like sourdough) using the remnants of a previous sauce. Hence the claim that, "My eel sauce is 100 years old." Cut the *anago* into *neta* pieces for *nigiri sushi* garnishing with the eel sauce and sesame seeds.

## Sauce Decoration

Eel sauce decoration

Other sauces decoration

## *Ebi* (Shrimp):

To skewer, hold the shrimp straight in the left hand; using a bamboo skewer with the right hand slide the skewer on the underside of the shrimp down the center line between the shell and the flesh taking care not to damage the flesh.

Boiling:
To 2 gallons of water add 1/2 cup of rice vinegar and 1/4 cup salt. Boil the skewered shrimp for a few minutes to 80-90% of being cooked through then immerse in ice water. Peel the skin off keeping the tail intact. Adding vinegar and salt to the

boiling water helps to preserve the color and flavor of the shrimp. If shrimp is overcooked shrinking will occur. To peel, remove the triangle piece of shell at the tail then loosen the shell along the bottom right side, turn the skewer while holding the loosened shell then detach the lower left side of the shell and remove. Be sure to hold the tail in place while loosening the shell to prevent the tail from breaking off. After peeling the shrimp trim the tail and loose flesh at the head end then use a butterfly cut along the underside of the shrimp to lay it open.

Marinate the shrimp with a light sprinkle salt marinade (*furi-jio*) for 20 minutes. Rinse in fresh water, then immerse in a 1:1 vinegar/water solution for 2 minutes. Pat dry, wrap in absorbent paper, then refrigerate overnight; shrimp will keep up to one week in the refrigerator.
Freeze for long term storage.

## *Suzuki* (Striped Bass):

Striped Bass is similar to the Japanese fish *Izumi-dai*.
Clean in the same manner as *Tai* but remove the skin as well.
There are 2 kinds.
One is farm raised from freshwater; the other is wild from the ocean.

Note: '*Suzuki*' is a close relative to Striped Bass.

## *An-kimo* (Monk Fish Liver):

*Anko* - monk fish, *Kimo* - liver. De-vein the liver and remove the skin. Wash thoroughly with salt then wash with *sake*. Rinse the liver in fresh water after washing in the salt and *sake*. Wrap the liver in plastic wrap and roll into a cylinder then wrap again in aluminum foil. Puncture the package with a skewer to release any trapped air. Place in a steamer and steam for 30-40 minutes. Let cool then slice into disks and arrange on julienne cucumber then garnish with *yakumi* such as *momiji-oroshi* and green onion.
Finish with *ponzu* sauce and *wasabi*.

Choose *An-kimo* that is pink in color, not too dark, and fresh looking with no odor. De-vein using a knife carefully to prevent damaging the liver. Use a paper towel to help grasp the skin to pull it off the liver.

## Other Style of *Nigiri*

Barracuda illustrates how one fish can be served in a variety of ways. Filet in the standard fashion. Make *nigiri sushi* garnishing with grated ginger and soy sauce. Marinate one filet with *konbu* seaweed (*kobu-jime*); wipe down the *konbu* with a damp cloth. Moisten the *konbu* with steaming hot water then wrap in plastic wrap and allow cooling. When cooled and softened lay one piece flat on a tray, lay a fish filet on the *konbu* and another piece of *konbu* on the fish filet. Wrap up the layers in plastic wrap. Lay a second tray on top and place weight on the tray which will insure that the *konbu* flavor is transferred to the fish; refrigerate.

Cut *neta* pieces for *nigiri sushi* garnishing with soy sauce and a small piece of the *konbu*. *Kobu-jime* works well with any white fish, such as halibut and *tai*.

Another way to serve the barracuda is *tempura nigiri*. Dredge a *neta* piece in *tempura* flour, then *tempura* batter, then deep fry. Top with a 1:1 ratio of honey/plum sauce mixture. Or make *sushi* roll as described previously.

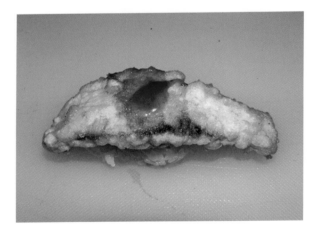

## Tsutsumi Sushi

*Tsutsumi sushi* is made with a wrapping technique. Lay two *neta* pieces side by side with their edges touching on cheese cloth or plastic wrap then layer a small ball of rice on the *neta* pieces; gather and twist the cloth or plastic wrap around the neta and rice to form a ball. Use *tai, toro, maguro, ebi* (butterfly cut with the tail removed). Make a *maguro, tai,* and *ebi* ball then skewer them together to serve.

To make *tsutsumi sushi* "flowers," form the *neta* pieces and rice as above but use more rice to get a larger sphere. Slightly flatten then push an indentation into the top to form a flower shape. Fill the indentation with *masago* for the flower center. Picture on left is shown from the back of the presentation.

Pictured here with assorted *sashimi*.

*Maguro tsutsumi sushi* with *inari sushi*:

The *inari* is stuffed with a rice mixture (rice, white and black sesame seeds, juice from the *tofu*), layer on egg sheet julienne, *masago* (2 colors), a piece of shrimp with tail, a cucumber half-round fan.

## *Hako Sushi* (Box Sushi):

*Hako sushi* with *shake* (salmon):

Moisten the box mold with water then lay in a piece of plastic *haran*. Cut the salmon in *nigiri* size pieces and layer them into the mold. Sprinkle a layer of *sarashi-negi* on the salmon then fill the mold with *sushi* rice. Or mix rice with sesame seeds, *sarashi-negi*, chopped *shiso* leaf, and or *masago* if desired. Place the top on the *sushi* mold then press rotating the mold two or three times to ensure an even pressing.

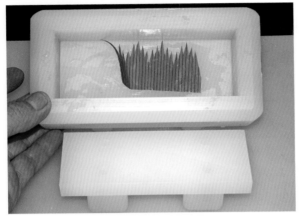
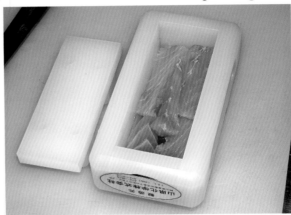

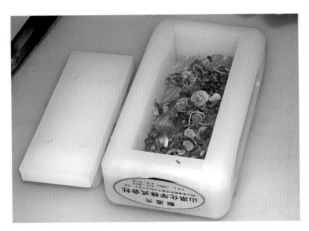
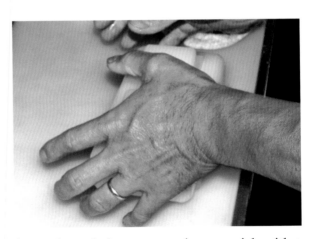

Remove the *sushi* from the mold and cut into six pieces, three pieces being one serving, garnish with *tera-kobu*. Or cut into 3/4 inch squares (12 pieces), garnish with *masago*, or a slice of jalapeño pepper, or green onion. Top with *wasabi* sauce and decorate with red chili sauce and radish sprouts.

*Hako sushi* with *maguro*:
Prepare the mold as with the salmon. Layer in the *neta* pieces of tuna and *sushi* rice. Press the *sushi* into shape and turn out of the mold. Cut the *sushi* into 12 pieces garnishing with *sarashi-negi*, capers, and mayonnaise.

*Hako sushi* with *saba* is called *Battera sushi*.
Cut a filet in 3 or 4 layers from the top of the flesh to the skin. Cut the last layer with the skin into *nigiri* size pieces. Moisten the box mold with water then lay in a piece of plastic *haran*, layer in a piece of *saba* with the skin side down the stomach section curled up the side of the mold to form an outside corner when the mold is removed. Complete the *saba* layer with pieces without skin. Layer 6 oz of rice over the *saba* and press. Turn out of the mold, top with a piece of pickled seaweed (*tera-kobu*), garnish with ginger and *ponzu*. Cut into 3/4 inch squares.

*Hako sushi* with shrimp:
Butterfly the shrimp, shell the tails, lay in the mold then layer in a little rice; lay in a piece of *nori* and *shiso* then layer in more rice and press.

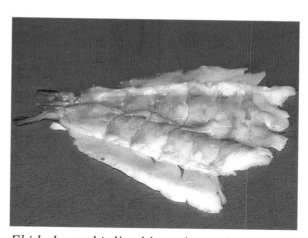

*Ebi hako sushi* sliced into six portions.

## *Chirashi Sushi*

Japanese style (traditional):
In a bowl place *sushi* rice, eel sauce, julienne *nori*, julienne *kinshi tamago* (egg sheet), julienne *daikon* in the back of the bowl, and *shiso* leaf on the *daikon*. *Ebi* is the main item so it is placed on the *shiso* leaf.

*Tamago neta*, crab stick, *hamachi*, *maguro*, *shake* (salmon), *tai* (in flower design), *masago*, *gari*, and *wasabi* are now added to the bowl.
Garnish with radish sprouts and a cucumber fan.

*Saiku sushi* is a creative dish made primarily for decoration and display. Partially split open a cuttlefish piece (from the body) between the top and bottom so you have two thin pieces hinged together.
Place a piece of *nori* (trimmed to fit) inside the cuttlefish then turn the piece over and slice through every 1/4 inch or so leaving a margin on one edge to hold all the pieces together creating a fan. Arrange on a *shiso* leaf supported by a bed of rice.

Modern style is made in a round metal mold, the mold is then removed and the *chirashi* is served on a round western style plate. Here rice is mixed with chopped cilantro (*shiso* leaf may also be used) and black sesame seeds. Next, pour a little eel sauce on the rice mixture followed by julienne *nori* and julienne *kinshi tamago* (egg sheet)

Now place *tamago* omelet pieces, a *shiso* leaf, *ebi*, *shake*, *maguro*, *tai*, *gari*, and *wasabi* decoratively on the rice and julienne. Remove the metal mold then decorate the plate with a cucumber fan and different colored sauces for interest and contrast.

Another *chirashi* example:

Mini *chirashi*:

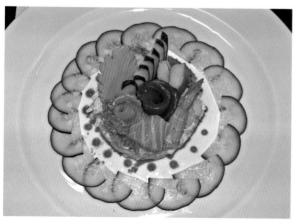

# *Uni*

## *Uni* (Sea Urchin):

*Uni* is alive if the spines respond with movement when touched. Remove the mouth using a shucking knife.

Then scrape out the five egg sections from inside using a spoon. Choose a heavy sea urchin to have more eggs inside. Place the eggs in an iced 5% salt water solution to rinse them. Rinse out the shell with fresh water then place julienne *daikon* inside.

Add cucumber garnish, *shiso* leaf, and the sea urchin eggs to complete the presentation.

## *Kai* (Clams):

- *Hokki-gai* (Surf clam)
- *Miru-gai* (Giant clam)
- *Aoyagi* (Orange clam)
- *Kaki* (Oyster)
- *Hotate-gai* (Scallop)

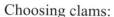

To prevent damaging the clam take care to slide the shucking knife along the inside wall of the shell.

Choosing clams:
The muscle should react by closing itself when the shell is squeezed. If the shell is excessively heavy it is full of mud or if the shell rattles when you shake it the muscle inside is dead. Only live calms are used for *sushi*.

## *Hotate-gai* (Scallop):

Using a shucking tool carefully cut along the interior side of the shell to remove the scallop and muscle. Cut the outer muscle off carefully taking care not to puncture the viscera. Pull the scallop free of the viscera, separate the liver, and then discard the remaining viscera. Immerse the muscle and the scallop 3 times in boiling water for 1 second or less. Immerse immediately after in ice water. Peel off any skin left on the scallop as well as any sand. Clean the muscle section then rinse in fresh water. The scallop and muscle can be used for *sushi* or *sashimi*. To use the scallop shell for serving or for decoration boil for 30 minutes in water then sun dry for one day.

Scallop *sushi* cutting:
Cut the scallop in half then cut each half partially through and butterfly open to make a *neta* piece.

## Green Muscles

Parboil 3 minutes then immerse in ice water. Pull the shells open; use the edge of the other shell to scrape the muscle off its attachment. Cut the muscle in half the long way then grill briefly over a flame then make *nigiri* and wrap with a *nori hachimaki*; finish with eel sauce.

## *Kaki* (Oyster):

To open insert the shucking knife into the shell on the flat side and loosen the muscle connection to the shell. Rinse in fresh water after opening.

Serve on the half shell with *ponzu*, lemon juice, *momiji-oroshi*, *sarashi-negi*, and *masago*. Or make *nigiri sushi* or serve as *gunkan*. For freshness, keep oysters in the 1/2 shell on ice.

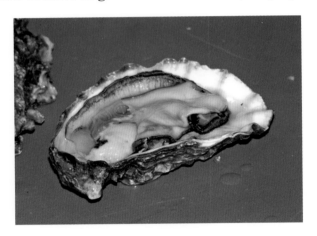

Full Moon Oyster Shooter:

In a champagne glass or shot glass place the oyster and *ponzu* sauce; add clear liquor such as *sake* or tequila if desired. Add *tobiko*, sriracha, citrus (*yuzu*, lemon, or lime juice), *sarashi-negi* and *momiji-oroshi*.

## *Miru-gai* (Giant Clam):

Remove the shell (be sure the shell is empty of water when you purchase the clam because at $20 per lb for clam any water trapped in the shell is weighed and purchased for $20 per lb). The shell can be boiled and dried in the sun for use in presentation.

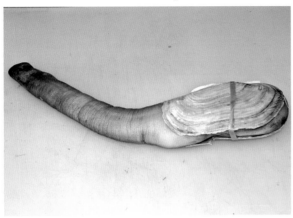

Cut away the viscera and fishy tasting soft meat from the muscle. The muscle and foot is parboiled 15-20 seconds then immersed in ice water. Wash the end of the foot with a brush or cloth.

Now peel off the skin then split the foot open length wise and clean out any sand. When cutting the clam for *nigiri* use a wiggle cut with the knife to get a wavy pattern on the face of the neta piece.

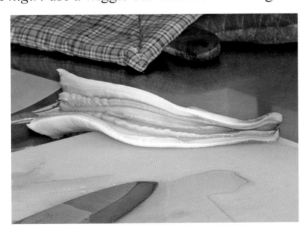
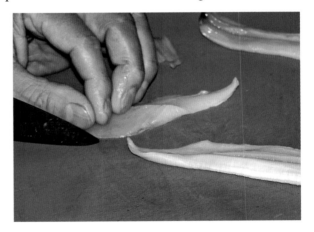

Slice the piece several times down one edge then place on the *nigiri* rice with *wasabi* and a cucumber slice. The cucumber will diminish the salty, fishy taste of the clam.

Wrap with a *nori* strip (*hachimaki*), top with sea salt and *yuzu* (citrus). If you slap the clam just before serving, it will be moving when served. (Slice the edge a little longer for more movement). *Miru-gai* is well complimented by cucumber which mellows the flavor. Cucumber is also a good compliment to oily summertime fish such as fresh and salt water eel.

## *Ko Ika* (Cuttlefish):

Rinse thoroughly in fresh water then use your fingers to loosen the head and tentacles. Remove the endo-skeleton and continue to loosen the head and tentacle section along the edges under the removed skeleton section. Pull the head and tentacles away from the body then remove the mouth, eyes, and ends of the longest tentacles then rinse well. Trim the body at the sides and across the top just part way through to facilitate removing all three layers of the skin. Use a cloth to help remove all the skin from the interior of the body. Rinse the body piece in fresh water then remove the skin from the fin sections. Parboil the fin sections and the tentacles; the body can be served raw.

## *Ama Ebi* (Sweet Shrimp):

Cut the head from the tail section then remove the shell. Peel the hard outer shell off of the head; peel off the tail shell then deep fry the head and tail shell. Dredge the head in flour before deep frying if desired. Display the head on the plate with the *nigiri*. Dry the head and tail shell before deep frying to prevent spattering of the oil. Cut along the top of the tail section flesh to de-vein then butterfly cut the tail and then immerse the tail in ice water. Make *nigiri sushi* with the tail section; garnish with fresh lemon juice and sea salt.

## *Ikura* (Salmon Eggs):

Place the frozen *ikura* in a bowl and rinse with fresh water then pour through a colander to strain. Remove the broken shells which taste bad. Rinsing also removes saltiness. Rinse again in *sake* which mellows the fishy taste. Then marinate the eggs in 1 part *dashi* - 1 part *mirin* - 1 part white soy sauce (*shiro* shoyu) for 2 days in a covered container in the refrigerator.

Here *ikura* is presented in a lime cut as a container with a lid.

## *Masago* (Smelt Eggs) and *Tobiko* (Flyingfish Eggs)

*Masago*

*Tobiko*

*Tobiko*

*Tobiko*

## Wa-gashi (Japanese Dessert):

*Shiratama* powder (rice starch) is mixed in equal parts with water and kneaded into a paste. Form into 3/4 inch balls and push a small indentation in the top and drop into boiling water for 3-5 minutes. They are done when they float to the surface. Then immerse in an ice water bath and pat dry. Mix some of the *shiratama* powder with green tea powder to make green colored balls or coat them with red bean paste.

### Zenzai:

Make 2 inch diameter disks with the *shiratama* paste. Place a pinch of red bean paste in the center of the disk and form the disk around the bean paste into a ball then drop into the boiling water. Immerse in ice water and pat dry. Roll the balls in black or white ground sesame seeds.

### Kinako:

Mix 2 Tbls soy bean powder in a bowl with 1 Tbls of sugar then roll the *shiratama* balls in the mixture. Red bean paste can also be diluted with water into a broth. The rice starch balls are then floated in the broth for a delicious dessert.

### Sweet *wa-gashi*:

Soak 2 pieces of dried *kanten* (agar-agar) for 10-15 minutes in water then cook about 10 minutes in 5 cups of water and 1 cup of sugar. The agar-agar will melt into solution. Strain about 25% of the liquid into a bowl and add 1 teaspoon green tea powder and mix well. Pour the mixture through a strainer into a rectangular mold then place in the refrigerator for 10-15 minutes. Be sure that all the bubbles have been removed from the surface of the liquid. Remove from the refrigerator when the liquid has set.

Score the surface of the agar- gar jell with a fork so the next layer will adhere. Layer on the 3/4 inch balls made of sweet red bean paste. Now pour in the last 75% of the agar-agar liquid (strain before pouring into pan) then place in the refrigerator for 20 minutes.

Here we put it all together into a delicious treat.

*Tempura* ice cream:
Wrap a scoop of ice cream in thin slices of pound cake being sure to cover all of the ice cream.
Wrap in plastic wrap and twist tightly to form a ball then freeze for a few minutes.
To cook, roll the ice cream balls in flour then in thick tempura batter and deep fry for 20-30 seconds.
Serve on the flower pedal orange and garnish with chocolate sauce.

# *Haran* Cutting

*Saiku sushi* (creative *sushi*) is used for visual effect; this includes various novelty *sushi* rolls and *haran* cutting.
Remove the spine from the back of the leaf, often bamboo, but other leaves work as well. Fold the leaf in half along the spine then cut into various shapes to unfold into a chosen design.
To keep, refrigerate in water.

# Sushi Case

*Sushi (Neta)* Case:

The *neta* case is decorated in the 'Mt. Fuji' style, that is, the fish is presented in the *neta* case so that the design flows to the center from each side. The tuna and the more expensive fish are displayed in the center of the *neta* case on 'Mt. Fuji.' This design reflects the seating on the customer side of the *sushi* bar where the center of the *sushi* case is the focal point. Five people per *sushi* chef is considered the 'optimum maximum,' that is around 50 pieces of *sushi* for the chef to prepare.

In conclusion,

I have wanted to create a school text book since the beginning. Creating a book from scratch is no simple task…Many people, much sacrifice and time was required to make this dream a reality. I would like to extend a special thanks to William McLane for his effort and support.

This book is not just showing how to make sushi; it is a real traditional and fundamental education for basic Japanese cooking and sushi making. Now people are able to learn Japanese cuisine in an efficient and effective manner. Why would I want to share our secret recipes and techniques? Here are my reasons:

Japanese food is good for the body, the mind and the soul. A healthy human has a more peaceful and overall better quality of life. I would like sushi chefs to make safe, nutritious, beautiful and great tasting sushi and other Japanese cuisine. Understanding Japanese cooking brings us closer to Mother Nature; this healthy way of life makes a safer and prosperous environment for us and our children. We need to keep our land healthy and peaceful for future generation. Japanese cuisine makes great chefs and great people! Simple, Season and Sublime; these are the foundation to Japanese cuisine.

Last but not least I would like to say thanks to our staff members; Mr. Yosuke Ouchi, Mr. Nick Kang and other associates. I couldn't have come this far without their support.

However, we need to keep our goals grand; one down, one million to go!

*Chef Andy F. Matsuda*
*C.E.O*
*Sushi Chef Institute*

# Appendix: Photograph Gallery

Dishes created by:
Chef Andy Matsuda
of Sushi Chef Institute

Photographs by:
Bruce James and Jennifer James
James and James Photography

# Appendix: Terminology

*Hocho*: Knife
*Yanagi*: *Sushi*/*Sashimi* knife
*Deba*: Cleaver for whole fish cutting
*Usuba*: Vegetable knife
*Kasumi*: The edge made from two type of metal
*Hon'yaki*: 100% Carbon steel knife

*To-ishi*: Whet Stone
*Ara-to*: Coarse grade #800
*Naka-to*: Medium grade #1000
*Shiage-togi*: Fine grade #2000-3000
*Men-naoshi*: Headache stone
*Sabi-tori*: Eraser

*Nabe*: Pot
*Tamago-yaki-ki*: Egg pan

*Hashi*: Chopsticks
*Wari-bashi*: Disposable chopsticks
*Sai-bashi*: Decoration chopsticks
*Mori-bashi*: Decoration chopsticks
*Ten-bashi*: *Tempura* chopsticks
*Kana-gushi*: Steel skewer
*Take-gushi*: Bamboo skewer

*Me-uchi*: Eel spikes
*Hone-nuki*: Bone picker
*Kai-ake*: Shucker
*Uroko-hiki*: Scaler
*Kawa-muki-ki*: Peeler
*Makisu*: *Sushi* bamboo mat

*Oroshi-gane*: Grater
*Suri-bachi*: Grinding bowl
*Atari-bo* (*Suri-kogi*): Grinding stick
*Ura-goshi*: Sieve
*Jogo*: Funnel
*Mushi-kan*: Steam pan
*Nagashi-kan*: Steam mold
*Haran* (*Baran*): Leaf for decorations

*Shoyu*: Soy sauce
*Koikuchi Shoyu*: Regular soy sauce
*Usukuchi Shoyu*: Light soy sauce
*Tamari Shoyu*: *Tamari* soy sauce
*Shiro Shoyu*: White soy sauce
*Tosa Shoyu*: *Tosa* soy sauce
*Ponzu Shoyu*: Citrus soy sauce

*Shio*: Salt
*Ara-jio*: Sea salt

*Sato*: Sugar

*Mirin*: Sweet rice wine

*Sake*: *Sake*
*Sake-kasu*: *Sake* sediment after filtration

*(O-)Su*: Vinegar

*Abura*: Oil
*Goma-abura*: Sesame oil

*Goma*: Sesame seed
*Sansho*: Sichuan pepper
*Kuro Kosho*: Black pepper
*Shiro Kosho*: White pepper
*Karashi*: Mustard paste
*To-garashi*: Red pepper

*Ichi-mi To-garashi*: Chili pepper 1 flavor
*Shichi-mi To-garashi*: Chili pepper 7 flavors
*Yuzu-Kosho*: Salt-cured green chili spiced *yuzu*
*Goma-Shio*: Sesame and salt
*Shio-Kosho*: Salt and pepper

*Shiro-miso*: White *miso*
*Aka-miso*: Red *miso*

*Katakuri-ko*: Potato starch
*Komugi-ko*: Flour
*Pan-ko*: Japanese breadcrumb

*San-mai-oroshi*: 3 pieces cut
*Go-mai-oroshi*: 5 pieces cut

*Tate-jio*: Salt water marinate
*Furi-jio*: Light salt sprinkle marinate
*Beta-jio*: Heavy salt marinate

*Shimo-furi*: Sear by hot water
*Yaki-shimo*: Sear by fire

*Kobu-jime*: Kelp marinate
*Zuke*: Marinated tuna in soy sauce


*Yakumi*: Condiment
*Negi*: Green onion
*Shiso* (*Oba*): Perilla leaf
*Shoga*: Ginger
*Wasabi*: *Wasabi* radish

*Daikon-oroshi*: Grinded *daikon*
*Momiji-oroshi*: Grinded *daikon* with chili
*Oroshi-shoga*: Grinded ginger
*Sarashi-negi*: Chopped and washed green onion

*Daikon*: White radish
*Gobo*: Burdock
*Ninjin*: Carrot
*Tama-negi*: Onion

*Kabocha*: Japanese squash
*Kyuri*: Cucumber

*Horenso*: Spinach
*Hakusai*: Napa cabbage
*Kaiware*(*-daikon*): *Daikon* sprout

*Gen-mai*: Brown rice
(*O-*)*Kome*: Rice


*Kinoko*: Mushroom
*Enoki*(*-take*): *Enokitake* mushroom
*Matsu-take*: *Matsutake* mushroom
*Shi-take*: *Shitake* mushroom


*Daidai*: Japanese sour orange
*Yuzu*: *Yuzu* citron


*Tsuke-mono*: Pickles
*Gari*: Pickled ginger
*Takuan*: Pickled *daikon*
*Yama-gobo*: Pickled burdock


*Kanten*: Agar-agar
*Koya-dofu*: Dry frozen *tofu*
*Tofu*: *Tofu*

*Aji*: Spanish mackerel
*Ama-ebi*: Sweet shrimp
*Anago*: Sea eel
*Awabi*: Abalone
*Ebi*: Shrimp
*Fugu*: Blow fish
*Hamachi*: Yellowtail
*Hamaguri*: Cherry stone clam
*Hirame*: Halibut
*Hotate-gai*: Scallop
*Ika*: squid
*Ise-ebi*: Lobster
*Iwashi*: Sardine
*Kaki*: Oyster
*Kamasu*: Barracuda
*Kani*: Crab
*Karei*: Flounder
*Katsuo*: Skip jack bonito
*Kohada*: Gizzard shad
*Koi*: Carp
*Maguro*: Tuna
*Miru-gai*: Giant clam
*Masago*: Smelt egg
*Saba*: Jack mackerel
*Shake* (*Sake*): Salmon
*Sawara*: King mackerel
*Suzuki*: Sea bass
*Tai*: Sea bream
*Tako*: Octopus
*Tobiuo*: Flying fish
*Unagi*: Fresh water eel
*Uni*: Sea urchin
*Tobiko*: Flying fish egg

*Kani-kama*(*boko*): Imitation crab meat

*Ao-nori*: Nori flakes
*Katsuo-bushi*: Bonito flakes
*Konbu*: Kelp
*Kisami-nori*: Fine julienne seaweed
*Nori*: Seaweed
*Wakame*: *Wakame*

u-Verb
*Furu*: Sprinkle
*Hiku*: Pull / Grind
*Hitasu*: Soak
*Iru*: Roast, Toast
*Kezuru*: Shave
*Kiru*: Cut, Slice
*Kizamu*: Chop, Mince
*Kosu*: Strain
*Kosuru*: Rub
*Kudaku*: Crumble
*Mabusu*: Coat, Dust
*Muku*: Peel
*Musu*: Steam
*Nuru*: Brush
*Orosu*: Grate
*Saku*: Tear
*Samasu*: Chill, Cool
*Sarasu*: Soak, Rinse
*Sasu*: Skewer
*Shiboru*: Wring, Squeeze
*Suru*: Grind
*Taku*: Cook
*Tokasu*: Dissolve
*Toku*: Beat
*Toru*: Take, Remove
*Tsubusu*: Mash
*Yaku*: Bake, Broil, Grill, Roast

ru-Verb
*Ageru*: Deep-fry
*Atatameru*: Heat
*Itameru*: Sauté, Stir-fry, Brown
*Kuwaeru*: Add
*Mazeru*: Ross, Mix, Blend, Stir, Combine
*Niru*: Simmer, Braise, Cook, Boil
*Tsukeru*: Dip, Soak
*Yuderu*: Boil, Parboil

Irregular Verb
*Suru*: Do
*Kuru*: Come
*Aru*: Be, Exist

*Irasshai mase*: Welcome!
*Arigato gozai mashita*: Thank you

*Itadaki masu*: (Before you eat)
*Oishi desu*: Taste good
*Go-chiso sama deshita*: (After you eat)

*Ohayo gozai masu*: Good morning
*Konnnichi wa*: Hello
*Konban wa*: Good evening
*O-genki desu ka?*: How are you?
*Sayonara*: Good-bye
*Oyasumi nasai*: Good night

*O-tsukare sama deshita*: Thank you for working together
*Domo / Arigato*: Thanks
*Sumimasen*: Excuse me
*Gomen nasai*: I am sorry

*Hai*: Yes
*"E-E-A"*: No

# Appendix: Food Cost

Restaurant operation costs are 25% food costs, 25% rent or lease, 25% staff, 5% overhead (insurance, utilities, etc), and 20% maximum profit.

Therefore, the basic rule of thumb is 4 times the food cost is the price to the consumer.

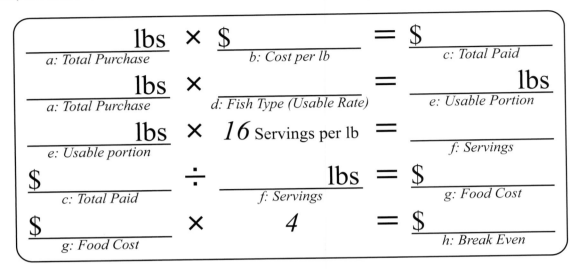

### Albacore (loin):
| | | |
|---|---|---|
| 3 lbs | × $6.75 per lb | = $20.25 |
| 3 lbs | × 1.00 | = 3 lbs |

(Very little waste or loss)

| | | |
|---|---|---|
| 3 lbs | × *16* Srvs per lb | = 48 Servings |
| $20.25 | ÷ 48 Servings | ≒ $0.43 per Serving |
| $0.43 | × 4 | = $1.72 (Break Even) |

Sold at $4.00 per Serving with $2.28 profit

### Salmon (whole):
| | | |
|---|---|---|
| 25 lbs | × $4.75 per lb | = $118.75 |
| 25 lbs | × 0.80 | = 20 lbs |

(20% loss)

| | | |
|---|---|---|
| 20 lbs | × *16* Srvs per lb | = 320 Servings |
| $118.75 | ÷ 320 Servings | ≒ $0.38 per Serving |
| $0.38 | × 4 | = $1.52 (Break Even) |

Sold at $4.00 per Serving with $2.48 profit

### Toro:
| | | |
|---|---|---|
| 20 lbs | × $28 per lb | = $560 |
| 20 lbs | × 0.70 | = 14 lbs |

(30% loss)

| | | |
|---|---|---|
| 14 lbs | × *16* Srvs per lb | = 224 Servings |
| $560 | ÷ 224 Servings | = $2.50 per Serving |
| $2.50 | × 4 | = $10 (Break Even) |

Sold at $10.00 per Serving with no profit

### Tuna:
| | | |
|---|---|---|
| 10 lbs | × $12 per lb | = $120 |
| 10 lbs | × 0.80 | = 8 lbs |

(20% lost in cutting blood line and skin)

| | | |
|---|---|---|
| 8 lbs | × *16* Srvs per lb | = 128 Servings |
| $120 | ÷ 128 Servings | ≒ $0.94 per Serving |
| $0.94 | × 4 | = $3.76 (Break Even) |

Sold at $4.00 per Serving with little profit

### Yellowtail:
| | | |
|---|---|---|
| 5 lbs | × $10 per lb | = $50 |
| 5 lbs | × 0.65 | = 3.25 lbs |

(35% +/- loss)

| | | |
|---|---|---|
| 3.25 lbs | × *16* Srvs per lb | = 52 Servings |
| $50 | ÷ 52 Servings | ≒ $0.97 per Serving |
| $0.97 | × 4 | = $3.88 (Break Even) |

Sold at $4.00 per Serving with little profit

### Halibut:
| | | |
|---|---|---|
| 4 lbs | × $6.75 per lb | = $27 |
| 4 lbs | × 0.50 | = 2 lbs |

(50% loss)

| | | |
|---|---|---|
| 2 lbs | × *20* Srvs per lb | = 40 Servings |

(Halibut is sliced thinner; 20 Servings per lb)

| | | |
|---|---|---|
| $27 | ÷ 40 Servings | ≒ $0.68 per Serving |
| $0.68 | × 4 | = $2.72 (Break Even) |

Sold at $4.00 per Serving with $1.28 profit

$$(Break\ Even) = \frac{(Cost\ per\ lb)}{4\ or\ 5 \times (Usable\ Rate)}$$

4 or 5; "5" is for Halibut
(Serving number per Lbs divided by 4)

$$(Servings) = 16\ or\ 20 \times (Total\ Purchase\ lbs) \times (Usable\ Rate)$$

16 or 20; "20" is for Halibut (Serving number per Lbs)

**Albacore (loin) - Very little loss:**

$$(Break\ Even) = \frac{\$6.75\ per\ lb}{4 \times 1.00} \doteqdot \$1.69$$

$$(Servings) = 16 \times 3\ lbs \times 1.00 = 48\ Srvs$$

**Salmon (whole) - 20% loss:**

$$(Break\ Even) = \frac{\$4.75\ per\ lb}{4 \times 0.80} \doteqdot \$1.49$$

$$(Servings) = 16 \times 25\ lbs \times 0.80 = 320\ Srvs$$

**Toro - 30% loss:**

$$(Break\ Even) = \frac{\$28\ per\ lb}{4 \times 0.70} = \$10$$

$$(Servings) = 16 \times 20\ lbs \times 0.70 = 224\ Srvs$$

**Tuna - 20% loss:**

$$(Break\ Even) = \frac{\$12\ per\ lb}{4 \times 0.80} = \$3.75$$

$$(Servings) = 16 \times 10\ lbs \times 0.80 = 128\ Srvs$$

**Yellowtail - 35% +/- loss:**

$$(Break\ Even) = \frac{\$10\ per\ lb}{4 \times 0.65} \doteqdot \$3.85$$

$$(Servings) = 16 \times 5\ lbs \times 0.65 = 52\ Srvs$$

**Halibut - 50% loss:**

$$(Break\ Even) = \frac{\$6.75\ per\ lb}{5 \times 0.50} = \$2.70$$

$$(Servings) = 20 \times 4\ lbs \times 0.50 = 40\ Srvs$$

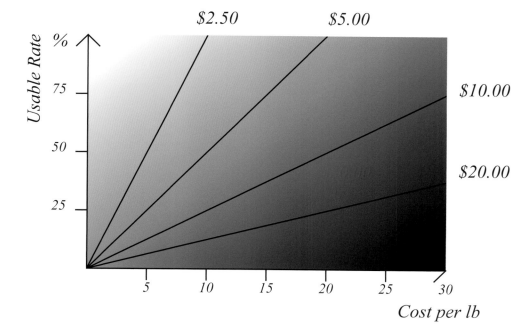

Graph of Break Even line by Cost (per lb) and Usable Rate (%)

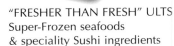

# TAKAOKAYA

**Purveyors of Quality Nori and Green Tea**